12.9b

CASABLANCA

Script and Legend

THE **50**TH ANNIVERSARY EDITION

CASABLANCA

Script and Legend

HOWARD KOCH

Preface by Howard Koch
Introductory Note to The First Edition
by Ralph J. Gleason
Foreword by Richard Brown
Essays by Howard Koch, Charles Champlin,
Richard Corliss, Roger Ebert, Umberto Eco,
Aljean Harmetz and J. Hoberman
Reviews by Howard Barnes and Bosley Crowther
Screenplay by Julius J. Epstein,
Philip G. Epstein and Howard Koch

AURUM PRESS

First published in Great Britain 1992 by Aurum Press Ltd,
10 Museum Street, London WC1A 1JS

First published in the United States by
The Overlook Press, New York

A catalogue record for this book is available
from the British Library

ISBN 1 85410 227 3

1 3 5 7 9 10 8 6 4 2
1993 1995 1996 1994 1992

Printed in the USA

Grateful acknowledgment is made to reprint the following material: "Introduc
tory Note to the First Edition" Ralph J. Gleason, Copyright © 1971 by Chron-
icle Publishing Company. Foreword by Richard Brown, Copyright © 1992
by Richard Brown. "Thoughts on *Casablanca*" by Charles Champlin,
Copyright © 1992 by Charles Champlin. "An Analysis of the Film" by Richard
Corliss, Copyright © 1973 by Richard Corliss. "*Casablanca* at Fifty" by Roger
Ebert, Copyright © 1992 by Roger Ebert. "Round Up The Usual Suspects"
by Aljean Harmetz, Copyright © 1992 by Aljean Harmetz. "*Casablanca*: Cult
Movies and Intertextual Collage" from *Travels In Hyperreality*, Copyright ©
1986, 1967 by Umberto Eco, reprinted by permission of Martin Secker and
Warburg Limited:"On *Casablanca*" by J. Hoberman Copyright © 1992 by
J. Hoberman. Review of *Casablanca* by Howard Barnes, Copyright © 1942
by the New York Tribune, Inc., reprinted by permission. Review of *Casablanca*
by Bosley Crowther, Copyright © 1942 by The New York Times Company,
reprinted by permission.

Film stills courtesy of The Museum of Modern Art, New York, NY, and
reproduced by arrangement with Turner Entertainment.

Cover design by Design Oasis

CONTENTS

PREFACE

AT PRESENT anyone with an eight- or sixteen-millimeter camera can become a movie maker—whether for his family and friends (a captive audience) or, hopefully, for a wider circle and possible commercial distribution. Responding to the demand of today's youth, most of our universities and colleges have courses on the technique of film-making. It has become open season for the aspiring amateur armed with an idea and enough raw stock to put it on film—and the whole world is his shooting ground.

Yet only a few decades ago motion picture production was the private preserve of a select group of professionals entrenched in a Pacific enclave called Hollywood, where art and commerce met head-on and tried to reconcile their conflicts as best they could. Hollywood Boulevard was not exactly paved with gold, but underfoot are the copper-inscribed names of those who mined it in vast quantities during its lush period—along with more fame than is usually accorded princes and presidents. Reigned over by a half dozen tycoons in an uneasy alliance with labor bosses of the closed craft unions, it was not an easy world to penetrate.

For a writer there was then no prescribed way of preparing for a career in films, as there was in the other arts and professions. It was largely a matter of chance. Some succeeded by virtue of a Broadway hit or a best-selling novel; others entered by the back door through a relationship—son, nephew, mistress, or whatever—with a studio executive, star, or powerful agent. Or if you were an expatriate Hungarian and adept at selling a story to a producer by acting it over a cocktail at Romanoff's, you might pry your way in, at least temporarily, until they discovered there was less to the story than met the ear. Perhaps no writer entered the heavily guarded studio gates under stranger circumstances than I. In a figurative sense, I arrived from outer space.

For six months I had been writing the radio plays for Orson Welles and John Houseman, co-producers of the Mercury Theatre. One of the scripts turned some unfriendly Martians loose on an unsuspecting public with results that have become part of American folklore. The vibrations were felt in Hollywood. Orson moved his Mercury team to Paramount while I was offered a contract at Warners.

Since it was the Hollywood custom to type-cast their writers as well as their actors, I posed a dilemma for the studio. What do you do with a writer—a very junior writer—whose specialty was assumed to be Martians? Fortunately, this was before science-fiction became fashionable or I might have been writing about out-of-space monsters for the rest of my literary life. While the story department debated my future—or more likely just forgot about me—I waited in my office, trying to get used to the unaccustomed luxury of drawing a salary for doing nothing. Eventually, through the intercession of a friend, John Huston, a producer was induced to give me a chance to dramatize an historical romance starring Errol Flynn and entitled *The Sea Hawk.* The picture succeeded (i.e., made money) and I moved to a psychological drama, *The Letter,* with William Wyler directing and Bette Davis starring. And then came *Casablanca.*

RALPH J. GLEASON

INTRODUCTORY NOTE
TO THE FIRST EDITION

THE OTHER NIGHT I dropped over to Rick's Place once more and found it had stood the years very well indeed.

"Rick's Place," for those of you who have been culturally deprived and are not familiar with one of the true romantic symbols of the World War II generation, more universally known I suspect than Harry's New York Bar, is the Café Américain in *Casablanca*.

And what I am talking about is the film *Casablanca,* with Ingrid Bergman, Humphrey Bogart, Dooley Wilson, and the rest. It was playing at the Telegraph Ave., Repertory Cinema and I couldn't resist such an excursion into pure, sweet nostalgia.

Casablanca was the film of my generation's youth, just as Bogart was the man and Ingrid Bergman the woman. Those were times when things were so much simpler; the good guys and the bad guys so much more clearly defined and the struggle itself, the moral imperative for man, so much more easily seen.

We had time for sentiment then. Was there a dry eye ever when Rick (interesting that over the years we remembered Bogart's name in the film was Rick but who remembered Bergman's was Ilsa?) gave the precious papers to Paul Henreid allowing him to take the lady and leave?

Casablanca summed up the morality of its time better, I think, than any other film ever has. Thirty years from now (*Casablanca* was set in North Africa in 1941) do you suppose that *Easy Rider* will look as good to today's young people grown then to middle age?

And Dooley Wilson, who played Sam, the Black pianist and singer who made ''As Time Goes By'' into the nostalgic theme of lost love for all of us, made his debut in that film with a background version of ''Shine'' (''just because my hair is curly, just because my teeth are pearly''), which even today's racially hip audiences miss.

Everybody saw *Casablanca*. Everybody knew the story, knew the characters, and knew the context. When, three years later, a radio specialist in the army Psychological Warfare branch wanted to let a friend in London know where he was, he started his letter from an APO address the way this column begins... ''The other night I dropped over to Rick's Place...'' and instantly his location was clear.

What a cast that was, too! Not only Bergman and Bogart as the lovers, but Peter Lorre, Sidney Greenstreet, and Claude Rains as the corrupt trio selling life to refugees in that terrible time after the fall of Paris.

And did any actor, including the great von Stroheim, ever play a Nazi officer with the precise arrogance and implicit evilness of Conrad Veidt? There were so many little touches: the Italian attaché and his eagerness to please; the resistance cadre headed by the character actor fresh out of *Ninotchka;* and the glorious German refugee waiter.

What made Bogart and Bergman so universal was their humanity, their vulnerability if you will. Bogart could afford to do a stupid thing, to be blind, and even to be supercilious. Bergman, well, all she had to do was to let those eyes fill with tears and the world was at her feet.

Surprisingly, the youthful Berkeley audience took *Casablanca* pretty much at face value. Now and then, especially in the scene where Bogart is sacrificing his own escape for Henreid and Bergman, the place was as quiet as a room full of living, breathing humans can be.

Now and then the sentimental parts provoked giggles or outright laughter, but it is hard, I suppose, to realize how sentiment can be real in another time and place. Delicate things like that are the first victims of changing times.

We could afford sentiment then, even in the darkest days of Hitler's victories. Is there sentiment now in revolutionary circles, one wonders?

But *Casablanca* was back then, before all the words and all the images became distorted, drained of their truth by broken promises and failed ambitions.

Peter Lorre, of course, has just the right touch of ratlike energy and deviousness as he begs for respect, but for me, the secondary character who is without peer is Sidney Greenstreet.

As in *The Maltese Falcon,* Greenstreet's role could be played by no one else before or since. His size, that huge portly figure, is an asset, but it isn't just the size, it is the stance.

Sidney Greenstreet had the kind of presence that implied knowledge of all the rituals of affluence, intimacy with the practice of power, and a direct, analytical mind that saw the world (and acted in that vision) as being governed ultimately by the forces of evil implicit in man since Cain.

Having Greenstreet run one cafe, the Blue Parrot (echoes of Sam Spade and the prior film) wherein the black market flourished and man was without honor even in misery, and Bogart run the other, where a kind of range rider mixture of compassion and amorality prevailed, was brilliant.

Bogart was the beautiful American expatriate, sportsman's honor, hard on the surface but sentimental inside. Loyal to his friends and above all to his employees, reserving judgments, capable of swift and violent action and of the quixotic gesture, the romantic self-sacrifice.

Casablanca was how we thought we were, all right, a pure explication of the mood in which we entered World War II and a greater distance than Mars even from the way we eventually came out of it, seduced by power, corrupted by affluence.

It was good to go back again in time to those days when, despite all our faults, we still believed in our own basic virtue. If today we are lost and by the wind grieved, it helps some to see us at a time when we were not, when the hope of truth and good and a positive affirmation was not so far away as the grim reality of today makes them seem.

Casablanca was not very far in time or space from Spain and its spirit ranged on through the first few years that followed with the Maquis and the resistance until Algeria and Indochina and the rest brought down a backdrop of the kind of reality that makes the dreams harder to have any more.

The sentiment is rarer now and the whole visible world has a kind of institutionalized concrete dimness instead of the sparkle of life it had when Rick could let her go a second time, losing her forever in a cause that meant more than the lives of three little people in Casablanca.

RICHARD BROWN

FOREWORD

AT FIRST GLANCE, *Casablanca* did not have the makings of a box-office success, let alone a celluloid classic. Even its original title—*Everybody Comes to Rick's*—left much to be desired. But a lot of elements—including a fortuitous name change—came beautifully together, and on November 27, 1942, when the film was released it had a topicality and immediacy that producer Hal Wallis and director Michael Curtiz could not have envisioned. The Allies had begun their major landing in Africa and the name "Casablanca" was suddenly everywhere.

It was a publicist's dream come true. But *Casablanca* did not become a classic because of its topicality or its title. This movie had a lot going for it: a terrific script, superb direction and great stars, but above all, this movie had *chemistry*. The chemistry between Bogart and Bergman was so thick it would make movie history. Some would say it defined movie romance for all time. The gentle, irresistible beauty of Bergman's smile played against Bogart's rugged visage seemed to fix—in a single image—what a love affair *ought* to be. The two of them together were quietly explosive. What is more, *Casablanca* established a new film principle that although physical beauty was important in our ideal woman, we looked for other qualities in our ideal man. Bogart was a far cry from the handsome—even beautiful—men who had dominated the screen during the previous two decades: Rudolph Valentino, John Barrymore, Douglas Fairbanks, Jr. Yet there was something in Bogart's manner and presence that appealed to both men and women on a visceral level.

Casablanca's appeal was more than just visual. The words of *Casablanca* have worked their way into our language perhaps more insistently than those of any other Hollywood movie: it is surely one of the most quoted—and misquoted—movies of all time. Even fifty years later, ''We'll always have Paris,'' ''Here's looking at you, kid,'' and ''Play it again, Sam,'' instantly conjure up a poignant picture of lost love. (Any devotee will tell you that the last of these legendary lines occurs neither in the original script nor the finished movie. What Rick actually says to Sam is a simple, anguished ''Play it.'')

The song Rick and Ilsa can't resist hearing again is, of course, ''As Time Goes By.'' Although now one cannot think of the song apart from the film, ''As Time Goes By'' was not written for *Casablanca*. It was, in fact, a standard written over a decade earlier. The legendary Max Steiner, who had labored over a magnificent score, strongly resented the inclusion of the song in *his* film. And it might never have made it into the finished film—except for a haircut.

''As Time Goes By'' was written in 1931 by Herman Hupfeld for the show *Everybody's Welcome*. Max Steiner, who had created a splended musical score for *Casablanca,* considered the song intrusive in the film. New music might have simply been laid over the old—but for one problem. Dooley Wilson, who did not play piano (he was in fact a ''singing-drummer''), had synchronized his own ''make-believe playing'' to a record of the song in ''playback'' on the set. So any new music would have been clearly out-of-synch.

Eventually, however Steiner prevailed, and the producers agreed to re-shoot the scenes completely. Preparations were made and the actors were called back. But then the plan fell apart. Bergman had just cut her hair for the role of Maria in *For Whom The Bell Tolls*, so the new shots would not have matched. The notion was abandoned, and *Casablanca* went on to make this obscure little song a musical icon — a wistful emblem of unfulfilled possibilities for all time.

If *Casablanca* defined true love for a generation of incurable romantics, it also defined the aesthetic possibilities of cinema for a generation of film lovers. Beneath the irresistible passion was an intricate framework of creative elements and hard work which formed the foundation of *Casablanca*. The gifted artists who came together on this project produced a complex and ambitious cinematic feast. Good versus evil, true love versus expediency and tomorrow's war headline versus nostalgia for "the way it used to be" combined in a rich and heady brew. It is somehow fitting that the success story of the film itself represents the kind of happy ending we have come to expect from a classic Hollywood movie.

The film's beginnings were inauspicious to say the least. A New York high school teacher named Murray Bennett was visiting Europe in 1938 as the Nazis were tightening their grip on the continent. In a small café on the French Riviera teeming with a rich interntional cast of characters—Germans, French, English and a half dozen other nationalities—he saw a scene of desperation and fear starting to unfold before actual war had broken out. The star of Burnett's play, *Everybody Comes to Rick's,* was in fact the café, and it remains a key player in the finished film. Another element of inspiration from this real life café came in the form of a Black piano player. In the play and in the film Sam was Rick's friend and equal. As played by Dooley Wilson, he was a character with dignity and substance; this at a time when Black actors played Pullman porters and maids and got to tapdance occasionally. Here was one more element of integrity that enriched this ground-breaking film.

Casablanca was not intended to be a major Warner release; it was on the 1942 production schedule as a "B" movie. Clearly, it was a project that initially generated little enthusiasm. Directors Vincent Sherman and William Keighley turned the project down and finally Warner head Hal Wallis chose William Wyler to direct, but the project proved no more popular with this formidable director. Finally it fell to Michael Curtiz, a fine, workman-like director who was well-respected but in no sense one of Warner's start talents.

While casting negotiations and directorial changes were going on, Burnett's script was being worked on. Julius and Philip Epstein, Wally Kline, Howard Koch, Aeneas MacKenzie and Jerry Wald all contributed to the script. Julius Epstein had been a radio publicist and writer of one-act plays, Howard Koch had graduated from Columbia with a law degree and Murray Burnett was a high school teacher. Their collaboration made for as unlikely an alliance as the friendship between Captain Renault and Rick Blaine. But the results were equally fortuitous. Unlike the author of the play—who was very much a novice—the Epstein brothers, who worked on the script in its early stages, were skilled wordsmiths who effectively laid the foundation for what was to become perhaps the most memorable and best-loved Hollywood movie of all time.

In assessing the collaborative success of *Casablanca,* where so many elements came so perfectly together, one has to wonder how many times over the past fifty years a film lover has sat for the first time watching in awe as this affecting and elegant story unfolds, as the creative efforts of the film's many contributors gracefully combine to seduce and enchant. And one has to wonder how many times a film lover has emerged from the theater, still enveloped by the fog at the airport, still under movie's spell, and; anticipating a next visit to *Casablanca* has thought happily, ''This is the start of a beautiful friendship.''

RICHARD BROWN is a leading film scholar and executive director of The New York Center for Motion Picture Arts. He hosts the American Movie Classics cable network show ''Reflections on the Silver Screen'' which features his acclaimed interviews with actors and directors, and his famous film classes and seminars, which director Richard Attenborough has called ''the highlight of any trip to America,'' brings together guest speakers from the heart of the film industry.

THE MAKING OF CASABLANCA

HOWARD KOCH

A S IT APPROACHES its fifth decade, *Casablanca* shows little sign of aging or diminishing popularity. Since its original release it has played more revival dates than any other film in motion picture history. Although it is not an art film in the usual sense, it is shown consistently year after year in art and university theaters over the country. More articles have been written about it than any other picture with the possible exception of *Citizen Kane*. At the University of Illinois it is the subject of a thesis for a master's degree. "Rick's place" was used as a military code for the city of Casablanca in World War II. Restaurants and nightclubs in many cities have been named for the film and one in Philadelphia has actually duplicated the set of Rick's "Café Américain." The title of the Broadway play and motion picture by Woody Allen, *Play It Again, Sam,* needed no footnote to explain its origin. Everyone knew it was taken from *Casablanca* even though the actual words in the film were simply "Play it." (Ilsa says "Play it, Sam.") No doubt the "again" simply underlined the average person's nostalgic memory of the scene (so familiar on posters and on the covers of film anthologies) in which Bogart sits drinking in the closed café while Dooley Wilson sings, "As Time Goes By."

Yet none of us involved in its production could have foretold that *Casablanca* was to have an illustrious future—or, in fact, any future at all. Conceived in sin and born in travail, it survived its precarious origin by some fortuitous combination of circumstances to become the hardiest of Hollywood perennials, as tough and durable as its anti-hero, Humphrey Bogart.

It all began when Warners purchased the rights to a play entitled *Everybody Goes to Rick's,* which fell by the wayside before it reached Broadway. The play provided an exotic locale (later to become newsworthy by reason of the Casablanca conference of Roosevelt and Churchill) and a character named Rick who ran a café where most of the action in the screen story takes place. In addition to Bogart the studio had a superb cast on call that included Paul Henreid, Claude Rains, Peter Lorre, Sidney Greenstreet, Dooley Wilson, and Conrad Veidt. However, Jack Warner and his production head, Hal Wallis, wanted a new face for the female lead instead of one of the familiar feminine starts on the studio roster. Their selection of Ingrid Bergman, a Swedish actress beginning her Hollywoood career, turned out to be a felicitous choice. She possessed the personal qualities needed to portray the romantic idealist with conviction and without sentimentality and her slight accent lent authenticity to the character's middle-European background.

But at the time Miss Bergman was "owned" under the terms of a long contract by David Selznick and could only be pried away by the lure of a good story that would advance her career and her box-office value to the Selznick organization. Having nothing on paper to submit, Hal Wallis astutely dispatched Julius and Philip Epstein, two talented and fast-talking screenwriters, to Mr. Selznick, relying on them to improvise at least the semblance of an important story. They must have given quite a performance, because Selznick was sufficiently impressed to loan Miss Bergman.

But now the troubles really began. The Epsteins confessed to Wallis that the "story" with which they had entertained Mr. Selznick was actually a feat of verbal hocus-pocus without any real substance to provide a basis for a picture. Since the scheduled shooting date was only six weeks off, when the stars' costly salaries would begin, the news produced one of the crises so prevalent in Hollywood. The studio's method in such circumstances was to assign an additional writer or writers. I had just finished *The Letter,* so I was summoned to the front office and told to get to work on a film project entitled *Casablanca,* which had an imposing cast waiting in the wings and an accomplished director of action pictures, Michael Curtiz—in short, all the elements for a first-class production except the central ingredient, a story.

My collaboration with the Epstein brothers was entertaining and productive. They came up with all sorts of amusing lines for the various characters that were to people Rick's nightclub while I tried to fit the bits and pieces of plot into a dramatic continuity. Then one day after a week or so, my collaborators failed to appear. The Epsteins had been called to Washington on an emergency war service assignment.

The morning I heard the news was not one of my happiest moments. In the movie world there is no substitute for success and no acceptable excuse for failure. The Epsteins' work, before and after our brief collaboration, had provided a wealth of incidents, atmospheric bits and characterizations but they were not in any final continuity.

With the deadline creeping up on me and with Mike Curtiz asking when was he going to get pages, a kind of paralysis came over. I remember sitting in my corner office of the writers' building, staring out the window at the yellow-blooming acacia trees for one whole day. There was a mockingbird in the tree and, if you've got a mockingbird, you don't need any other because he has the whole repertoire of bird songs. This one had even added the flirtatious whistle that he'd probably picked up from some sailor on the make for a pretty girl. Or was the bird mocking me for wasting a precious day as though I expected a story to fly in through the open window?

On my desk, sharpened by my patient secretary, were a dozen brown pencils, Eagle Number One. I'd learned to have great respect for these pencils and use them to this day. Sometimes they seemed to take off on their own with me merely holding them, like the marker on a ouija board. The pencil obediently wrote down the two words that open every screen play—*Fade In.*

But fade in on what? Obviously the first thing was to establish the atmosphere. Fortunately, the Epsteins had done their research well and had bequeathed me some lively and often humorous incidents that graphically evoked the time and place. Casablanca was Moslem and during the Second World War it was a way station for refugees fleeing from German-occupied Europe to neutral countries. And it was notoriously corrupt. There was little distinction between the Vichy authorities who were supposed to enforce the laws and the criminals who made a living by breaking them. They were two sides of the same coin and often worked profitably together. As in Saigon of the Sixties, anything could be bought and sold on the black market—foreign currency, jewels, visas, girls, even human lives.

Once the atmosphere is established, the story must begin to move. I went through the rich assembly of actors waiting to take their parts in the story and picked Peter Lorre (Ugarte) as the one to initiate the action. With his round baby face and wide, bulging eyes Peter could mask his deviousness under a self-mocking innocence. Like his partner in crime, Ferrari, played by Sidney Greenstreet, he is a natural to be involved in black-market operations. In his opening scene we learn that he has acquired two letters of transit signed by General Weygand, granting the bearer the right to travel without passport or visa. He entrusts them to Rick for safekeeping until he can dispose of them at a fancy price. But two German couriers have been killed and we suspect that Ugarte has engineered their murder to gain possession of the valuable letters. A high Nazi official, Strasser, played by Conrad Veidt, has arrived in Casablanca accompanied by several subordinates. To impress the Germans, whom he secretly despises, Renault makes a big show of arresting Ugarte in their presence while dining in Rick's café. Ugarte, trying to escape, shoots at one of the police but is overpowered and presumably taken out to be executed.

As I come to this scene, I remind myself to play down the melodrama, letting the incident cause a minimum of commotion in the café—to give the impression that violence is endemic to wartime Casablanca. As after a shower quickly over and forgotten, the music and dancing resume and life goes on at Rick's as though nothing has happened.

The next question presents itself and the answer should open up new possibilities. Why has a Nazi official as important as Strasser come to Casablanca? Not just to insure the arrest of the man who killed the German couriers. He must obviously be after bigger game. Now is the time to plant the expected arrival of Strasser's antagonist—a man we must project as the crusading leader of Europe's anti-Nazis, by name Victor Laszlo and to be played by Paul Henreid. After escaping from a concentration camp, he has so far succeeded in eluding capture by the Germans. Although Casablanca is nominally unoccupied territory, the Germans control it through their Vichy stooges and Strasser warns Renault that Laszlo must never leave Casablanca, at least not alive.

Rick is our lead. Where does he stand at this point? Although Strasser's dossier reveals that Rick fought for the Loyalists during the fascist invasion of Spain, he professes no interest in politics. In the Ugarte incident he took a neutral position and, when questioned by Renault, he dismisses the subject: "I stick my neck out for nobody."

But by now we have also planted a woman with Laszlo, presumably his wife or mistress. And stories being what they are, the woman will be, of course, Ilsa (Ingrid Bergman), with whom Rick had the romantic affair in Paris.

Two weeks away from the scheduled shooting date, I recall taking stock of where we were (the "we" including the Epsteins, whose material I used in the sequence along with my own). Numerically, we had about forty pages, a quarter of the eventual screenplay. They were typed and sent to Curtiz, who quickly responded with enthusiasm, although I think Mike was so worried and hungry for a script that any pages would have looked good to him. The forty pages were mimeographed and sent to the various departments—casting, camera, set construction, montage, location, music, and special effects—that were assigned to the production.

From a story standpoint what did we have working for us at this juncture? In broad melodrama terms, we had established the bad guys (the Germans) and the good guy (Laszlo) and in an equivocal position between these extremes were Rick and Renault, both professedly cynical and out only for themselves. We also had a tangible stake—the letters of transit that had accidentally fallen into Rick's hands. I made a mental note that these could be useful later as the object of contention (how useful I didn't realize at the time). The dramatic question at the heart of the picture was beginning to emerge. How would Rick act in a crisis when confronted with unavoidable choice between taking one side or the other or, to put it another way, between his own interests and his real sympathies? Complicating that choice was a woman who had loved him and left him to share with Laszlo his life and his political mission. The structure of the film was at last taking shape.

The actors, of course, were aware that shooting was about to commence without a completed script. Ingrid Bergman, not as familiar with the studio system as the others in the cast, was concerned. She came to me and asked ''How can I play the love scene with Rick when I don't know whether I'm going to end with him or with Laszlo?'' I tried to reassure her although I was still not certain of the ending. With Humphrey Bogart and the others, they had been in the situation so often they took it in stride. At times when he sensed discouragement, Bogie would invite me into his dressing-room with his usual ''relax and have a drink.'' We would talk and sometimes a genie popped out of the whiskey bottle and off I'd go to develop the idea into a scene.

By the day shooting started, the first half was completed— about 65 pages of script—and to my astonishment, it seemed to be building, creating its own tensions, but there was still a long way to go. About two-thirds of the way through the production, it was a dead heat. I was getting the finished scenes down to the set on the morning they were to be shot. I received a memo from the front office reminding me that any day on which the cast had no material to shoot would cost the studio thirty thousand dollars. This warning didn't add to my peace of mind.

At the same time a new complication developed. During the initial stages, Curtiz, worried by the absence of a script, was so relieved to see pages accumulating that he accepted them without reservation or with slight modifications that were usually constructive. However, as the screenplay began to take its final shape, Mike was assailed by second thoughts and doubts. Accustomed to success on a certain level, he dreaded the possibility of a box-office failure.

In this uncertain state of mind he did what was so often the practice of producers and directors. He started giving out the incomplete script to various colleagues on the lot for their opinions. Inevitably, the reactions varied and Mike's attitude toward the emerging story shifted with the changing winds. I only discovered what was happening when revised pages came through from the stenographic department with changes I knew nothing about. Obviously Mike was scavenging ideas from sources unknown to me. When I protested that some of the changes were illogical and out of character, he would answer impatiently in his Hungarian idiom, ''Don't worry what's logical. I make it go so fast no one notices.''

As the distance between script and shooting narrowed and the pressures increased, our disagreements erupted into quarrels. I felt as though I were trying to design a solid structure while others were changing the blueprint in the course of construction. Mike, on his part, contended his directorial prerogatives were being challenged by a writer—and a writer not too well established at that.

From my present perspective I can be more objective. I realize the difference between us was mostly a matter of emphasis. Mike leaned strongly on the romantic elements of the story while I was more interested in the characterizations and the political intrigues with their relevance to the world struggle against fascism. Surprisingly, these disparate approaches somehow meshed and perhaps it was partly this tug-of-war between Curtiz and me that gave the film a certain balance.

One disagreement I remember arose over the flashback sequence in which Rich recalls his Paris love affair with Ilsa. I argued that these could only be conventional scenes with no dramatic progression until the end shot when Ilsa fails to show up at the railroad station. While they illustrated the cause of Rick's bitterness and cynicism, I felt that these were sufficiently exposed in the café scene with Ilsa. And I was afraid that the flashback would dissipate the tension that was building in the present.

However, in retrospect I suspect Mike was right. Probably at this point the romantic interlude was a useful retard and relief from tension—and the viewer needed some visual proof of the ardor of the love affair to be convinced of its profound effect on Rick. At any rate, Mike exercised his directorial prerogative and the sequence was written and shot in accordance with his ideas.

The final weeks were a nightmare of which I remember only fragments. When I sent down to the set the last scene and wrote *The End* on the screenplay, I felt like a weary traveler who had arrived at a destination but with only the foggiest notion where he was or how he had got there. In January, 1943, when the picture opened at Warner's Hollywood Theatre, I wondered what all the excitement was about. I was still blind to the virtues of the film and saw only what I considered its faults. When a year later it received the Academy Award, I was by that time inured to miracles.

In the course of the years many films have won Academy Awards. Also we can admit, without excess modesty, that there have been more profound films than *Casablanca*. On close examination we can find a number of inconsistencies and illogicalities. (I should know!) Judged as a realistic picture of political events in North Africa, it would fall far short of a film like *The Battle of Algiers*. Moreover, in these days when each action movie, whether western or war or crime, tries to outdo its predecessor in brutality and blood-letting, *Casablanca* is curiously lacking in overt violence. In only three scenes is there any gunplay and these are brief and understated. Most of the tension derives from dangers implicit in the situations and atmosphere and much of the conflict is in the realm of ideas. It would seem that the film retains its popularity not because it conforms to the contemporary mood but in spite of it. The essays that follow the screenplay examine the *Casablanca* mystique from the perspective of reviewers and scholars; yet perhaps equally important in assessing *Casablanca*'s place in film history is the devotion and loyalty it has inspired in film lovers around the world over the past fifty years.

THE
SCREENPLAY

JULIUS AND PHILIP EPSTEIN
AND HOWARD KOCH

Warner Bros. Pictures, Inc.
Presents

CASABLANCA

HUMPHREY BOGART
INGRID BERGMAN
PAUL HENREID
CLAUDE RAINS
CONRAD VEIDT
SYDNEY GREENSTREET
PETER LORRE
S. Z. SAKALL
MADELEINE LeBEAU
DOOLEY WILSON
JOY PAGE
JOHN QUALEN
LEONID KINSKEY
CURT BOIS

Producer   Hal B. Wallis
Director   Michael Curtiz
Play   Murray Burnett, Joan Alison
Screenplay   Julius J. Epstein, Philip G. Epstein,
Howard Koch
Photograph   Arthur Edeson
Film Editor   Owen Marks
Sound   Francis J. Scheid
Art Director   Carl Jules Weyl
Makeup   Perc Westmore
Set Decorations   George James Hopkins
Gowns   Orry-Kelly
Music   MAX STEINER

A LONG SHOT *of a revolving globe. As it revolves, lines of fleeing refugees are superimposed over it. Over this scene comes the voice of a narrator.*

NARRATOR

With the coming of the Second World War, many eyes in imprisoned Europe turned hopefully, or desperately, toward the freedom of the Americas. Lisbon became the great embarkation point. But not everybody could get to Lisbon directly; and so, a tortuous, roundabout refugee trail sprang up.

An animated map illustrates the trail as the narrator mentions the points.

NARRATOR

Paris to Marseilles, across the Mediterranean to Oran, then by train, or auto, or foot, across the rim of Africa to Casablanca in French Morocco. Here, the fortunate ones through money, or influence, or luck, might obtain exit visas and scurry to Lisbon, and from Lisbon to the New World. But the others wait in Casablanca, and wait, and wait, and wait.

A full shot of the old Moorish section of the city at daytime. At first only the turrets and rooftops are visible against a torrid sky. The camera pans down the facades of the Moorish buildings to a narrow, twisting street crowded with the polyglot life of a native quarter. The intense desert sun holds the scene in a torpid tranquility. Activity is unhurried. The narrator's voice fades away.

A police officer takes a paper from the typewriter. He turns to a microphone and reads.

OFFICER

To all officers! Two German couriers carrying important official documents murdered on train from Oran. Murderer and possible accomplices headed for Casablanca. Round up all suspicious characters and search them for stolen documents. Important!

A street in the old Moorish section. An officer blows his whistle several times. Native guards are rounding up people. Others are trying to escape. There is pandemonium. A police car full of officers screams through the street and stops in the market.

At a street corner two other policemen have stopped a white civilian and are talking to him.

1ST POLICEMAN

May we see your papers?

CIVILIAN
nervously

I don't think I have them on me.

1ST POLICEMAN

In that case, we'll have to ask you to come along.

CIVILIAN

patting his pockets

Wait. It's just possible that I...
Yes, here they are.

He brings out his papers. The 2nd policeman examines them.

2ND POLICEMAN

These papers expired three weeks ago. You'll have to come along.

Suddenly the civilian breaks away and starts to run wildly down the street. The policeman shouts "Halt!," but the civilian keeps going, at one point passing Jan and Annina Brandel, a refugee Bulgarian couple. A shot rings out, and the man falls under a large poster of Marshal Petain which reads: "Je tiens mes promesses, même celles des autres." The policemen frantically search the body merely to find Free France literature against the Vichy government.

An inscription, "Liberté, Egalité, Fraternité," is carved in a marble block along the roofline of a building. The camera pans down the facade, French in architecture, to the high-vaulted entrance over which is inscribed, "Palais de Justice." The camera continues to pan down to the entrance, where the arrested suspects are being led in by the police.

A sidewalk café on one side of the square. A middle-aged English couple are sitting at a table observing the commotion in front of the prefecture. A dark-visaged European, sitting at a table nearby, is watching the English couple more closely than the scene on the street.

ENGLISHWOMAN

What on earth's going on there?

ENGLISHMAN

I don't know, my dear.

DARK EUROPEAN

Pardon, pardon, M'sieur, pardon Madame, have you not heard?

ENGLISHMAN

We hear very little, and we understand even less.

DARK EUROPEAN

Two German couriers were found murdered in the desert.
with an ironic smile
The unoccupied desert. This is the customary roundup of refugees,
liberals, and uh, of course, a beautiful young girl for M'sieur Renault,
the Prefect of Police.

Across the street, in front of the Palais de Justice, refugees are
unloaded from the police van.

DARK EUROPEAN

Unfortunately, along with these unhappy refugees the scum of Europe
has gravitated to Casablanca. Some of them have been waiting years
for a visa.
puts his arms compassionately around the Englishman
I beg of you, M'sieur, watch yourself. Be on guard. This place is
full of vultures, vultures everywhere, everywhere.

ENGLISHMAN
a little taken aback by this sudden display of concern

Ha, ha, thank you, thank you very much.

DARK EUROPEAN

Not at all. Au revoir, M'sieur. Au revoir, Madame.

He leaves. The Englishman, still a trifle disconcerted by the European's action, looks after him.

ENGLISHMAN

Au revoir. Amusing little fellow, what? Waiter!

As he pats his breast pocket there is something lacking.

ENGLISHMAN

Oh. How silly of me.

ENGLISHWOMAN

What, dear?

ENGLISHMAN

I've left my wallet in the hotel.

ENGLISHWOMAN

Oh.

Suddenly he looks off in the direction of the departed dark European, the clouds of suspicion gathering. But now, overhead, the drone of a low-flying airplane is heard. Heads look up.

A shot of an airplane overhead, its motor cut for landing. The refugees waiting outside the Palais de Justice follow the flight of the plane. In their faces is revealed one hope they all have in common, and the plane is the symbol of that hope.

Jan and Annina are looking up at the plane.

ANNINA
wistfully

Perhaps tomorrow we'll be on that plane.

Near the airport, the plane is swooping down past a neon sign on a building at the edge of the airport. The sign reads, "Rick's Café Américain."

As the plane lands, a swastika on its tail becomes visible.

The plane taxis to a group of people at the terminal. As it comes to a stop, soldiers march into a formation in front of it. In the group waiting is Captain Louis Renault, a French officer appointed by Vichy as Prefect of Police in Casablanca. He is a handsome, middle-aged Frenchman, debonair and gay, but withal a shrewd and alert official. With him are Herr Heinze, the German consul, Captain Tonelli, an Italian officer, and Lieutenant Casselle, Renault's aide.

When the plane door is opened, the first passenger to step out is a tall, pale German with a smile that seems more the result of a frozen face muscle than a cheerful disposition. On any occasion when Major Strasser is crossed, his expression hardens into iron. Herr Heinze steps up to him with upraised arms.

HEINZE

Heil Hitler.

STRASSER
with a more relaxed gesture

Heil Hitler.

They shake hands.

HEINZE

It is very good to see you again, Major Strasser.

STRASSER

Thank you. Thank you.

Heinze takes Strasser over to Renault.

HEINZE

May I present Captain Renault, Police Prefect of Casablanca. Major Strasser.

The two shake hands.

RENAULT
courteously, but with just a suggestion of mockery beneath his words

Unoccupied France welcomes you to Casablanca.

STRASSER
in perfect English, smiling

Thank you, Captain. It's very good to be here.

RENAULT

Major Strasser, my aide, Lieutenant Casselle.

As they acknowledge each other, Captain Tonelli barges in front of Casselle and salutes Strasser.

TONELLI

Captain Tonelli, the Italian service, at your command, Major.

STRASSER

That is kind of you.

Renault leads Strasser toward the edge of the airfield, where their cars await them. Heinze follows, with Casselle and Tonelli bringing up the rear, engaged in a heated exchange of words.

RENAULT

again the suggestion of a double-edged implication
You may find the climate of Casablanca a trifle warm, Major.

STRASSER

Oh, we Germans must get used to all climates, from Russia to the Sahara.
with a slight smile
But perhaps you were not referring to the weather.

RENAULT

sidesteps the implication with a smile
What else, my dear Major?

STRASSER

casually
By the way, the murder of the couriers, what has been done?

RENAULT

Realizing the importance of the case, my men are rounding up twice the usual number of suspects.

HEINZE

We already know who the murderer is.

STRASSER

Good. Is he in custody?

RENAULT

Oh, there is no hurry. Tonight he'll be at Rick's. Everybody comes to Rick's.

STRASSER

I have already heard about this cafe, and also about Mr. Rick himself.

Outside the entrance to Rick's, people are arriving. From the neon sign, seen earlier, the camera pans down to the door of the cafe. From inside we hear sounds of music and laughter. The song is ''It Had to Be You.''

Inside, Rick's is an expensive and chic nightclub which definitely possesses an air of sophistication and intrigue. The camera pans around the room soaking in the atmosphere. An orchestra is playing. The piano is a small, salmon-colored instrument on wheels. There is a Negro on the stool, playing and singing. About him there is a hum of voices, chatter and laughter. The occupants of the room are varied. There are Europeans in their dinner jackets, their women beautifully begowned and bejeweled. There are Moroccans in silk robes. Turks wearing fezzes. Levantines. Naval officers. Members of the Foreign Legion, distinguished by their kepis.

A customer in the cafe, seated at a table.

MAN

Waiting, waiting, waiting. I'll never get out of here. I'll die in Casablanca.

A very well-dressed woman is talking to a Moor. She has a bracelet on her wrist, no other jewelry.

WOMAN

But can't you make it just a little more? Please.

MOOR

I'm sorry, Madame, but diamonds are a drug on the market. Everybody sells diamonds. There are diamonds everywhere. Two thousand, four hundred.

WOMAN

distressed
All right.

Two conspirators are talking.

1ST MAN

The trucks are waiting, the men are waiting. Everything is...

He stops talking as two German officers walk by.

Two men are sitting at a table.

MAN

It's the fishing smack Santiago. It leaves at one tomorrow night, here from the end of La Medina. Third boat.

REFUGEE

Thank you, oh, thank you.

MAN

And bring fifteen thousand francs in cash. Remember, in cash.

The camera dollies to the bar. As it passes the various tables we hear a babel of foreign tongues. Here and there we catch a scattered phrase or sentence in English. Now we are at the bar. The Russian bartender is a friendly young man. He hands a drink to a customer with the Russian equivalent of "Bottoms Up." The customer answers with "Cheerio."

Carl, the waiter, a fat, jovial German refugee with spectacles is walking, tray in hand, to a private door, over which a burly man stands guard.

CARL

Open up, Abdul.

ABDUL

respectfully, as he opens the door
Yes, Herr Professor.

Carl goes into the gambling room. The camera takes in the activity at the various tables. At one table two women are glancing offscene at Rick's table. One of them calls to Carl.

WOMAN

Uh, waiter.

CARL

Yes, Madame?

WOMAN

Will you ask Rick if he'll have a drink with us?

CARL

Madame, he never drinks with customers. Never. I have never seen him.

2ND WOMAN

disappointedly
What makes saloon-keepers so snobbish?

MAN

to Carl
Perhaps if you told him I ran the second largest banking house in Amsterdam.

CARL

The second largest? That wouldn't impress Rick. The leading banker in Amsterdam is now the pastry chef in our kitchen.

MAN

We have something to look forward to.

CARL

And his father is the bell boy.
laughs

The overseer walks up to a table with a paper in his hand. In the foreground at the table we see a drink and a man's hand. The overseer places a check on the table. The man's hand picks up the check and writes on it, in pencil: "Okay-Rick." The overseer takes the check. The camera pulls back to reveal Rick, sitting at a table alone playing solitary chess. There is no expression on his face. Rick is an American of indeterminate age. As people come into the gambling room, he nods approval to Abdul. Several people have just entered. The next man appears in the doorway. Abdul looks to Rick who is glancing toward the open door and indicating that the person seeking admittance is not to be let in. Abdul starts to close the door on the man.

ABDUL

I'm sorry sir, this is a private room.

GERMAN

Of all the nerve! Who do you think...? I know there's gambling in there! There's no secret. You dare not keep me out of here!

The man tries to push his way through the door as Rick walks up.

RICK

coldly
Yes? What's the trouble?

ABDUL

Er, this gentleman...

GERMAN

interrupting and waving his card
I've been in every gambling room between Honolulu and Berlin and if you think I'm going to be kept out of a saloon like this, you're very much mistaken.

At this moment, Ugarte tries to squeeze through the doorway blocked by the German. He gets through and passes Rick. He is a small, thin man with a nervous air. If he were an American, he would look like a tout.

UGARTE

Er, er, excuse me, please. Hello, Rick.

Rick just looks at the German calmly and takes the card out of the German's hand.

RICK

tearing up the card
Your cash is good at the bar.

GERMAN

What! Do you know who I am?

RICK

I do. You're lucky the bar's open to you.

GERMAN

This is outrageous. I shall report it to the Angriff!

The German storms off, tossing the pieces of his card into the air behind him. On his way back to his table, Rick meets Ugarte.

UGARTE

fawning
Huh. You know, Rick, watching you just now with the Deutsches Bank, one would think you'd been doing this all your life.

RICK

stiffening
Well, what makes you think I haven't?

UGARTE

vaguely
Oh, nothing. But when you first came to Casablanca, I thought...

RICK

coldly
You thought what?

UGARTE

fearing to offend Rick, laughs
What right do I have to think?
pulling out a chair at Rick's table
May I?
changing the subject
Too bad about those two German couriers, wasn't it?

RICK

indifferently
They got a lucky break. Yesterday they were just two German clerks; today they're the Honored Dead.

UGARTE

You are a very cynical person, Rick, if you'll forgive me for saying so.

RICK

shortly
I forgive you.

A waiter has just come up to the table with a tray of drinks. He places one before Ugarte.

UGARTE

Er, thank you.
to Rick
Will you have a drink with me please?

RICK

No.

UGARTE

I forgot. You never drink with...
to waiter
I'll have another, please.
to Rick, sadly
You despise me, don't you?

RICK

indifferently
If I gave you any thought, I probably would.

UGARTE

But why? Oh, you object to the kind of business I do, huh? But think of all those poor refugees who must rot in this place if I didn't help them. That's not so bad. Through ways of my own I provide them with exit visas.

RICK

For a price, Ugarte, for a price.

UGARTE

But think of all the poor devils who cannot meet Renault's price. I get it for them for half. Is that so parasitic?

RICK

I don't mind a parasite. I object to a cut-rate one.

UGARTE

Well, Rick, after tonight I'll be through with the whole business, and I am leaving finally this Casablanca.

RICK

Who did you bribe for your visa? Renault or yourself?

UGARTE

ironically
Myself. I found myself much more reasonable.
he takes an envelope from his pocket and lays it on the table
Look, Rick, do you know what this is? Something that even you have never seen.
lowers his voice
Letters of transit signed by General deGaulle. [Marshal Weygand] Cannot be rescinded, not even questioned.

Rick looks at him, then holds out his hand for the envelope.

UGARTE

One moment. Tonight I'll be selling those for more money than even I have ever dreamed of, and then, addio Casablanca! You know, Rick, I have many friends in Casablanca, but somehow, just because you despise me you're the only one I trust. Will you keep these for me? Please.

RICK

For how long?

UGARTE

Perhaps an hour, perhaps a little longer.

RICK

taking them
I don't want them here overnight.

UGARTE

Don't be afraid of that. Please keep them for me. Thank you. I knew I could trust you.

Ugarte leaves the table just as the waiter comes up.

UGARTE

Oh, waiter. I'll be expecting some people. If anybody asks for me, I'll be right here.

WAITER

Yes, M'sieur.

The waiter leaves. Ugarte turns to Rick.

UGARTE

Rick, I hope you are more impressed with me now, huh? If you'll forgive me, I'll share my good luck with your roulette wheel.

He starts across the floor.

RICK

Just a moment.

Ugarte stops. Rick comes up to him.

RICK

Yeah, I heard a rumor that those German couriers were carrying letters of transit.

Ugarte doesn't reply for a moment.

UGARTE

Huh? I heard that rumor, too. Poor devils.

Rick looks at Ugarte steadily.

RICK

slowly
Yes, you're right, Ugarte. I am a little more impressed with you.

Rick starts for the door.

In the cafe, Sam is playing and singing the ''Knock Wood'' number, accompanied by the orchestra. The cafe is in semi-darkness. The spotlight is on Sam, and every time the orchestra comes in on the ''Knock Wood'' business, the spotlight swings over to the orchestra. Rick makes his way from the gambling room to Sam on the floor. During one of the periods when the spotlight is on the orchestra, Rick slips the letters of transit into the piano.

Ferrari comes into the cafe, sits down and watches Sam in his number. He sees Rick. They smile at each other. At the end of the number, Ferrari goes to the bar to speak to Rick.

FERRARI

as he comes up to Rick
Hello, Rick.

RICK

Hello, Ferrari. How's business at the Blue Parrot?

FERRARI

Fine, but I would like to buy your cafe.

RICK

It's not for sale.

FERRARI

You haven't heard my offer.

RICK

It's not for sale at any price.

FERRARI

What do you want for Sam?

RICK

I don't buy or sell human beings.

FERRARI

That's too bad. That's Casablanca's leading commodity. In refugees alone we could make a fortune if you would work with me through the black market.

RICK

Suppose you run your business and let me run mine.

FERRARI

Suppose we ask Sam? Maybe he'd like to make a change.

RICK

Suppose we do.

FERRARI

My dear Rick, when will you realize that in this world today isolationism is no longer a practical policy?

Rick and Ferrari walk over to the piano.

RICK

Sam, Ferrari wants you to work for him at the Blue Parrot.

SAM

I like it fine here.

RICK

He'll double what I pay you.

SAM

Yeah, but I ain't got time to spend the money I make here.

RICK

Sorry, Ferrari.

At the long bar in the cafe proper, Yvonne is sitting on a stool drinking brandy, Sacha, who is looking at her with lovesick eyes, is filling her tumbler.

SACHA

The boss's private stock. Because, Yvonne, I loff you.

YVONNE

morosely
Oh, shut up.

SACHA

fondly
All right, all right. For you, Yvonne, I shot opp, because, Yvonne, I loff you. Uh oh.

Rick saunters into the scene, and leans against the bar next to Yvonne. He pays no attention to her. She looks at him bitterly, without saying a word.

SACHA

Oh, M'sieur Rick, M'sieur Rick. Some Germans, boom, boom, boom, boom, gave this check. Is it all right?

Rick looks the check over and tears it up. Yvonne, who has never taken her eyes off Rick, finally blurts out:

YVONNE

Where were you last night?

RICK

his back is to her
That's so long ago, I don't remember.

A pause

YVONNE

Will I see you tonight?

RICK

matter-of-factly
I never make plans that far ahead.

Yvonne turns, looks at Sacha, extends her glass to him.

YVONNE

Give me another.

RICK

Sacha, she's had enough.

YVONNE

Don't listen to him, Sacha. Fill it up.

SACHA

Yvonne, I loff you, but he pays me.

Yvonne wheels on Rick with drunken fury.

YVONNE

Rick, I'm sick and tired of having you...

RICK

Sacha, call a cab.

SACHA

Yes, boss.

RICK

taking Yvonne by the arm
Come on, we're going to get your coat.

YVONNE

Take your hands off me!

He pulls her along toward the hall door.

RICK

No. You're going home. You've had a little too much to drink.

On the street in front of Rick's Sacha stands at the curb signaling a cab. Finally one pulls up. Rick and Yvonne come out of the cafe. He is putting a coat over her shoulders. She is objecting violently.

YVONNE

Who do you think you are, pushing me around? What a fool I was to fall for a man like you.

RICK

to Sacha, as he and Yvonne approach the waiting cab
You'd better go with her, Sacha, to be sure she gets home.

SACHA

Yes, boss.

RICK

And come right back.

SACHA

his face falling
Yes, boss.

Rick is now standing outside the cafe, looking up at the revolving beacon light from the airport, which intermittently sheds its light on *Rick's face. In the foreground, Renault is seated at a table on the cafe terrace.*

RENAULT

Hello, Rick.

RICK

walking over to him
Hello, Louis.

RENAULT

How extravagant you are, throwing away women like that. Someday they may be scarce.

Rick sits down at the table.

RENAULT

his eyes are amused
You know, I think now I shall pay a call on Yvonne, maybe get her on the rebound, eh?

RICK

When it comes to women, you're a true democrat.

As they talk, Captain Tonelli and Lieutenant Casselle walk by to enter the cafe. Casselle is talking non-stop; Tonelli tries.

RENAULT

If he gets a word in it'll be a major Italian victory.

Rick laughs. There is the sound of an airplane on the adjacent airfield. Rick and Renault look in its directions. The plane takes off and flies directly over their heads.

RENAULT

The plane to Lisbon.
a pause
You would like to be on it?

RICK

curtly
Why? What's in Lisbon?

RENAULT

The clipper to America.

Rick doesn't answer. His look isn't a happy one.

RENAULT

I have often speculated on why you don't return to America. Did you abscond with the church funds? Did you run off with a senator's wife? I like to think you killed a man. It's the romantic in me.

RICK

still looking in the direction of the airport.
It was a combination of all three.

RENAULT

And what in heaven's name brought you to Casablanca?

RICK

My health. I came to Casablanca for the waters.

RENAULT

Waters? What waters? We're in the desert.

RICK

I was misinformed.

RENAULT

Huh!

Emil, the croupier, comes out of the cafe and walks over to Rick.

EMIL

Excuse me, M'sieur Rick, but a gentleman inside has won twenty thousand francs. The cashier would like some money.

RICK

not at all perturbed
Well, I'll get it from the safe.

EMIL

I am so upset, M'sieur Rick. I do not understand how...

RICK

Forget it, Emil. Mistakes like that happen all the time.

The three men enter the cafe and walk through, passing Sam at the piano.

RENAULT

Rick, there's going to be some excitement here tonight. We are going to make an arrest in your cafe.

RICK

somewhat annoyed
What, again?

RENAULT

This is no ordinary arrest. A murderer, no less.

Rick's eyes react. Involuntarily, they glance toward the gambling room.

RENAULT

who has caught the look
If you are thinking of warning him, don't put yourself out. He cannot possibly escape.

RICK

I stick my neck out for nobody.

RENAULT

A wise foreign policy.

They start upstairs to Rick's office, passing Casselle who is still haranguing Tonelli.

RENAULT

You know, Rick, we could have made this arrest earlier in the evening at the Blue Parrot; but out of my high regard for you we are staging it here. It will amuse your customers.

RICK

Our entertainment is enough.

As Renault speaks, Rick is opening up the safe in a small dark room off the office. From the angle of the shot, only Rick's shadow can be seen, getting the money out.

RENAULT

Rick, we are to have an important guest tonight, Major Strasser of the Third Reich, no less. We want him to be here when we make the arrest. A little demonstration of the efficiency of my administration.

RICK

I see. And what's Strasser doing here? He certainly didn't come all the way to Casablanca to witness a demonstration of your efficiency.

RENAULT

Perhaps not.

RICK

giving the money to Emil
Here you are.

EMIL

It shall not happen again, M'sieur.

RICK

That's all right.

Emil exits.

RICK

Louis, you've got something on your mind. Why don't you spill it?

RENAULT

admiringly
How observant you are. As a matter of fact, I wanted to give you a word of advice.

RICK

Yeah? Have a brandy?

RENAULT

Thank you. Rick, there are many exit visas sold in this cafe, but we know that you have never sold one. That is the reason we permit you to remain open.

RICK

amiably
I thought it was because we let you win at roulette.

RENAULT

Er, that is another reason. There is a man who's arrived in Casablanca on his way to America. He will offer a fortune to anyone who will furnish him with an exit visa.

RICK

Yeah? What's his name?

RENAULT

Victor Laszlo.

RICK

Victor Laszlo!

RENAULT

watching Rick's reaction
Rick, that is the first time I have ever seen you so impressed.

RICK

casual, again
Well, he's succeeded in impressing half the world.

RENAULT

It is my duty to see that he doesn't impress the other half.
now intensely serious.
Rick, Laszlo must never reach America. He stays in Casablanca.

RICK

It'll be interesting to see how he manages.

RENAULT

Manages what?

RICK

His escape.

RENAULT

Oh, but I just told you...

RICK

Stop it. He escaped from a concentration camp and the Nazis have
been chasing him all over Europe.

RENAULT

This is the end of the chase.

RICK

Twenty thousand francs says it isn't.

They sit.

RENAULT

Is that a serious offer?

RICK

I just paid out twenty. I'd like to get it back.

RENAULT

Make it ten. I am only a poor corrupt official.

RICK

Okay.

RENAULT

Done. No matter how clever he is, he still needs an exit visa, or I should say, two.

RICK

Why two?

RENAULT

He is traveling with a lady.

RICK

He'll take one.

RENAULT

I think not. I have seen the lady. And if he did not leave her in Marseilles, or in Oran, he certainly won't leave her in Casablanca.

RICK

Maybe he's not quite as romantic as you are.

RENAULT

It doesn't matter. There is no exit visa for him.

RICK

Louis, whatever gave you the impression that I might be interested in helping Laszlo escape?

RENAULT

Because, me dear Ricky, I suspect that under that cynical shell you're at heart a sentimentalist.

Rick makes a face.

RENAULT

Oh, laugh if you will, but I happen to be familiar with your record. Let me point out just two items. In 1935 you ran guns to Ethiopia. In 1936, you fought in Spain on the Loyalists' side.

RICK

And got well paid for it on both occasions.

RENAULT

The winning side would have paid you much better.

RICK

Maybe.
changing the subject
Well, it seems you are determined to keep Laszlo here.

RENAULT

I have my orders.

RICK

Oh, I see. Gestapo spank.

RENAULT

My dear Ricky, you overestimate the influence of the Gestapo. I don't interfere with them and they don't interfere with me. In Casablanca I am master of my fate. I am captain of my...

He stops short as his aide enters and speaks.

AIDE

Major Strasser is here, sir.

RICK

as Renault starts to leave
Yeah, you were saying...?

RENAULT

hurriedly
Excuse me.

He hurries away. Rick smiles cynically.

Downstairs again, Renault walks up to Carl.

RENAULT

Carl, see that Major Strasser gets a good table, one close to the ladies.

CARL

I have already given him the best, knowing he is German and would take it anyway.

Renault walks over to one of his officers.

RENAULT

in a low voice
Take him quietly. Two guards at every door.

OFFICER

Yes, sir. Everything is ready, sir.

He salutes and goes off to speak to the guards. Rick has just come down the stairs. Renault walks over to Strasser's table.

RENAULT

Good evening, gentlemen.

STRASSER

Good evening, Captain.

HEINZE

Won't you join us?

RENAULT

sitting down
Thank you. It is a pleasure to have you here, Major.

STRASSER

to the waiter
Er, champagne and a tin of caviar.

RENAULT

Er, may I recommend Veuve Cliquot '26, a good French wine.

STRASSER

Thank you.

WAITER

Very well, sir.

STRASSER

A very interesting club.

RENAULT

Especially so tonight, Major.
in a low voice
In a few minutes you will see the arrest of the man who murdered
your couriers.

STRASSER

I expected no less, Captain.

*In the gambling room Ugarte is standing at the roulette table with
his back to the camera. Two gendarmes approach him from behind.*

GENDARME

Monsieur Ugarte?

UGARTE

looking around
Oh. Yes?

GENDARME

Will you please come with us.

UGARTE

Certainly. May I first please cash my chips?

The officer nods, the two follow Ugarte to the Cashier.

UGARTE

as he puts his chips through the window.
Pretty lucky, huh? Two thousand, please.

At the door to the gambling room, two guards have just stationed themselves in case there is trouble.

CASHIER

Two thousand.

UGARTE

Thank you.

Ugarte starts to walk out, followed by the gendarmes. At the doorway, he suddenly rushes through and slams the door behind him. By the time the gendarmes manage to get the door open again, Ugarte has pulled a gun. He fires at the doorway. The shots bring on pandemonium in the cafe. As Ugarte runs through the hallway he sees Rick, appearing from the opposite direction, and grabs him.

UGARTE

Rick! Rick, help me!

RICK

Don't be a fool. You can't get away.

UGARTE

Rick, hide me. Do something! You must help me, Rick. Do something!

Before he can finish, guards and gendarmes rush in and grab Ugarte. Rick stands impassive as they drag Ugarte off.

UGARTE

Rick! Rick!

STRASSER

still seated at his table, to Renault
Excellent, Captain.

Rick is still standing where he was, as a customer walks by.

MAN

half kiddingly, half earnest
When they come to get me, Rick, I hope you'll be more of a help.

RICK

I stick my neck out for nobody.

Rick comes out on the floor. An air of tense expectancy pervades the room. A few customers are on the point of leaving. Rick speaks in a very calm voice.

RICK

I'm sorry there was a disturbance, folks, but it's all over now.
Everything's all right. Just sit down and have a good time. Enjoy
yourself.
glances toward Sam
All right, Sam.

Sam nods and begins to play.

Renault, Strasser and Heinze are at their table. Rick walks by.

RENAULT

calling to Rick
Oh, Rick?

Rick stops and comes over to the table.

RENAULT

Rick, this is Major Heinrich Strasser of the Third Reich.

STRASSER

How do you do, Mr. Rick?

RICK

Oh, how do you do?

RENAULT

And you already know Herr Heinze of the Third Reich.

Rick nods to Strasser and Heinze.

STRASSER

Please join us, Mr. Rick.

Rick sits at the table.

RENAULT

We are very honored tonight, Rick. Major Strasser is one of the reasons the Third Reich enjoys the reputation it has today.

STRASSER

smiling
You repeat ''Third Reich'' as though you expected there to be others.

RENAULT

Well, personally, Major, I will take what comes.

STRASSER

to Rick
Do you mind if I ask you a few questions? Unofficially, of course.

RICK

Make it official, if you like.

STRASSER

What is your nationality?

RICK

pokerface
I'm a drunkard.

RENAULT

That makes Rick a citizen of the world.

RICK

I was born in New York City if that'll help you any.

STRASSER

amiably
I understand you came here from Paris at the time of the occupation.

RICK

There seems to be no secret about that.

STRASSER

Are you one of those people who cannot *imagine* the Germans in their beloved Paris?

RICK

It's not particularly *my* beloved Paris.

HEINZE

Can you imagine us in London?

RICK

When you get there, ask me.

RENAULT

Ho, diplomatist!

STRASSER

How about New York?

RICK

Well, there are certain sections of New York, Major, that I wouldn't advise you to try to invade.

STRASSER

Aha. Who do you think will win the war?

RICK

I haven't the slightest idea.

RENAULT

Rick is completely neutral about everything. And that takes in the field of women, too.

Strasser takes a little black book from his pocket and turns to a certain page.

STRASSER

You weren't always so carefully neutral. We have a complete dossier on you.
reads
"Richard Blaine, American. Age, thirty-seven. Cannot return to his country."
looks up from the book
The reason is a little vague. We also know what you did in Paris, Mr. Blaine, and also we know why you left Paris.

Rick reaches over and takes the book from Strasser's hand.

STRASSER

Don't worry. We are not going to broadcast it.

RICK

looking up from the book
Are my eyes really brown?

STRASSER

You will forgive my curiosity, Mr. Blaine. The point is, an enemy of the Reich has come to Casablanca and we are checking up on anybody who can be of any help to us.

RICK

with a glance toward Renault
My interest in whether Victor Laszlo stays or goes is purely a sporting one.

STRASSER

In this case, you have no sympathy for the fox?

RICK

Not particularly. I understand the point of view of the hound, too.

STRASSER

Victor Laszlo published the foulest lies in the Prague newspapers until the very day we marched in, and even after that he continued to print scandal sheets in a cellar.

RENAULT

Of course, one must admit he has great courage.

STRASSER

I admit he is very clever. Three times he slipped through our fingers. In Paris he continued his activities. We intend not to let it happen again.

RICK

rises with a slight smile

You'll excuse me, gentlemen. Your business is politics. Mine is running a saloon.

STRASSER

Good evening, Mr. Blaine.

Rick walks away toward the gambling room.

RENAULT

You see, Major, you have nothing to worry about Rick.

STRASSER

Perhaps.

At the entrance of the cafe, a couple is just coming in. They are Victor Laszlo and his companion, known as Miss Ilsa Lund. She wears a simple white gown. Her beauty is such that people turn to stare. The headwaiter comes up to them.

HEADWAITER

Yes, M'sieur?

LASZLO

in quiet, even tones
I reserved a table. Victor Laszlo.

HEADWAITER

Yes, M'sieur Laszlo. Right this way.

IB-1

As the headwaiter takes them to a table, they pass by the piano, and the woman looks at Sam. The latter, with a conscious effort, keeps his eyes on the keyboard. The camera stops on Sam. After she has gone out of the scene, Sam steals a look in her direction. A man soon to be identified as Berger observes the couple. Strasser and Renault look up from their table. The headwaiter seats Ilsa. Laszlo takes the chair opposite. He surveys the room.

LASZLO

Two cointreaux, please.

WAITER

Yes, M'sieur.

LASZLO

to Ilsa
I saw no one of Ugarte's description.

ILSA

Victor, I, I feel somehow we shouldn't stay here.

LASZLO

If we would walk out so soon, it would only call attention to us. Perhaps Ugarte's in some other part of the cafe.

A slight, middle-aged man, Berger, walks up to their table.

BERGER

Excuse me, but you look like a couple who are on their way to America.

LASZLO

Well?

Berger takes a ring from his finger.

BERGER

You will find a market there for this ring. I am forced to sell it at a great sacrifice.

LASZLO

Thank you, but I hardly think...

BERGER

Then perhaps for the lady. The ring is quite unique.

He holds it down for their view. Carefully lifting up the stone, he reveals, on a gold plate in the setting underneath, an impression of the Lorraine Cross of General deGaulle.

LASZLO

Oh, yes, I'm *very* interested.

BERGER

Good.

LASZLO

lower voice
What is your name?

BERGER

Berger, Norwegian, and at your service, sir.

LASZLO

to Berger, in a low voice

I'll meet you in a few minutes at the bar.
in a louder voice, obviously for the benefit of someone offscene
I do not think we want to buy the ring. But thank you for showing
it to us.

Berger takes the cue. He sighs and puts the ring away.

BERGER

Such a bargain. But that is your decision?

LASZLO

I'm sorry. It is.

*As Berger walks away, he brushes by Captain Renault who is ap-
proaching the table. He glances sharply at Berger as he passes. Then
he beams toward the table.*

RENAULT

Monsieur Laszlo, is it not?

LASZLO

Yes.

RENAULT

I am Captain Renault, Prefect of Police.

LASZLO

Yes. What is it you want?

RENAULT

amiably
Merely to welcome you to Casablanca and wish you a pleasant stay. It is not often we have so distinguished a visitor.

LASZLO

Thank you. You'll forgive me, Captain, but the present French administration has not always been so cordial. May I present Miss Ilsa Lund?

RENAULT

bows
I was informed you were the most beautiful woman ever to visit Casablanca. That was a gross understatement.

Ilsa's manner is friendly and reserved, her voice low and soft.

ILSA

You are very kind.

LASZLO

Won't you join us?

RENAULT

If you will permit me.
calls to the waiter
Oh, Emil. Please, a bottle of your best champagne, and put it on my bill.

EMIL

Very well, sir.

LASZLO

No, Captain, please.

RENAULT

No. Please, M'sieur, it is a little game we play. They put it on the bill, I tear the bill up. It is very convenient.

Ilsa laughs and glances off in Sam's direction.

ILSA

Captain, the boy who is playing the piano, somewhere I have seen him.

RENAULT

Sam?

ILSA

Yes.

RENAULT

He came from Paris with Rick.

ILSA

Rick? Who's he?

RENAULT

smiling
Mademoiselle, you are in Rick's and Rick is, er...

ILSA

Is what?

RENAULT

Well, Mademoiselle, he's the kind of a man that, well, if I were a woman and *I*...
tapping his chest
...were not around, I should be in love with Rick. But what a fool I am talking to a beautiful woman about another man.

Renault stops and looks off, then jumps to his feet as Strasser enters.

RENAULT

Er, excuse me. Ah, Major. Mademoiselle Lund, Monsieur Laszlo, may I present Major Heinrich Strasser.

Strasser bows and smiles pleasantly.

STRASSER

How do you do. This is a pleasure I have long looked forward to.

There is not the slightest recognition from either Ilsa or Laszlo. Strasser waits to be asked to seat himself.

LASZLO

I'm sure you'll excuse me if I am not gracious, but you see, Major Strasser, I'm a Czechoslovakian.

STRASSER

You were a Czechoslovakian. Now you are a subject of the German Reich!

LASZLO

I've never accepted that privilege, and I'm now on French soil.

STRASSER

I should like to discuss some matters arising from your presence on French soil.

LASZLO

This is hardly the time or the place.

STRASSER

hardening
Then we shall state another time and another place. Tomorrow at ten in the Prefect's office, with Mademoiselle.

LASZLO

Captain Renault, I am under your authority. Is it your order that we come to your office?

RENAULT

amiably
Let us say that it is my request. That is a much more pleasant word.

LASZLO

Very well.

Renault and Strasser bow shortly.

RENAULT

Mademoiselle.

STRASSER

Mademoiselle.

As they walk away.

RENAULT

to Strasser
A very clever tactical retreat, Major.

Strasser looks at Renault sharply, but sees only a noncommittal smile on Renault's face.

At the table, Laszlo watches after Strasser and Renault.

LASZLO

This time they really mean to stop me.

ILSA

Victor, I'm afraid for you.

LASZLO

We have been in difficult places before, haven't we?

Ilsa smiles back at him, but her eyes are still troubled.

On the floor, Corina strums a guitar and begins her number. Meanwhile, Laszlo looks about him with apparent casualness. He sees Strasser and Renault whispering together, then Berger.

LASZLO

I must find out what Berger knows.

ILSA

Be careful.

LASZLO

I will, don't worry.

He rises and goes off. The camera closes in on Ilsa's troubled profile. While Corina is singing, Sam gives a worried glance in Ilsa's direction. Ilsa watches him.

At the bar, Berger is sipping a drink. Laszlo walks up, and casually takes a place at the bar next to Berger.

LASZLO

Mr. Berger, the ring, could I see it again?

BERGER

Yes, M'sieur.

LASZLO

to Sacha
A champagne cocktail, please.

Laszlo takes the ring and looks at it.

BERGER

in a low voice
I recognize you from the news photographs, M'sieur Laszlo.

LASZLO

In a concentration camp, one is apt to lose a little weight.

BERGER

We read five times that you were killed in five different places.

LASZLO

smiles wryly
As you see, it was true every single time. Thank heaven I found you, Berger. I am looking for a man by the name of Ugarte. He is supposed to help me.

BERGER

shakes his head silently
Ugarte cannot even help himself, M'sieur. He is under arrest for murder. He was arrested here tonight.

LASZLO

absorbs the shock quietly
I see.

BERGER

with intense devotion
But we who are still free will do all we can. We are organized, M'sieur, underground like everywhere else. Tomorrow night there is a meeting at the Caverne du Roi. If you would come...

He stops as he sees Sacha bringing the drink to Laszlo.

Corina finishes her song.

At Laszlo's table, Ilsa sits alone.

ILSA

to waiter
Will you ask the piano player to come over here, please?

WAITER

Very well, Mademoiselle.

Renault comes up to where Berger and Laszlo are sitting.

RENAULT

How's the jewelry business, Berger?

BERGER

Er, not so good.
to Sacha
May I have my check, please?

RENAULT

Too bad you weren't here earlier, M'sieur Laszlo. We had quite a bit of excitement this evening, didn't we, Berger?

BERGER

Er, yes. Excuse me, gentlemen.

LASZLO

My bill.

RENAULT

No. Two champagne cocktails, please.

SACHA

Yes, sir.

At Laszlo's table, Sam wheels in the piano. On his face is that funny fear. Ilsa herself is not as self-possessed as she tries to appear. There is something behind this, some mysterious, deep-flowing feeling.

ILSA

Hello, Sam.

SAM

Hello, Miss Ilsa. I never expected to see you again.

He sits down and is ready to play.

ILSA

It's been a long time.

SAM

Yes, ma'am. A lot of water under the bridge.

ILSA

Some of the old songs, Sam.

SAM

Yes, ma'am.

Sam begins to play a number. He is nervous, waiting for anything.

ILSA

Where is Rick?

SAM

evading
I don't know. I ain't seen him all night.

Sam looks very uncomfortable.

ILSA

When will he be back?

SAM

Not tonight no more. He ain't coming. He went home.

ILSA

Does he always leave so early?

SAM

Oh, he never...well...
desperately
he's got a girl up at the Blue Parrot. He goes up there all the time.

ILSA

You used to be a much better liar, Sam.

SAM

Leave him alone, Miss Ilsa. You're bad luck to him.

ILSA

softly
Play it once, Sam, for old time's sake.

SAM

I don't know what you mean, Miss Ilsa.

ILSA

Play it, Sam. Play ''As Time Goes By.''

SAM

I can't remember it, Miss Ilsa. I'm a little rusty on it.

Of course he can. He doesn't want to play it. He seems even more scared.

ILSA

I'll hum it for you.
starts to hum

He begins to play it very softly.

ILSA

Sing it, Sam.

And Sam sings.

SAM

''You must remember this,
A kiss is just a kiss,
A sigh is just a sigh,
Etc.''

The door to the gambling room opens. Rick comes swinging out. He has heard the music and he is livid. He walks briskly up to the piano.

RICK

Sam, I thought I told you never to play...

As he sees Ilsa, he stops abruptly, stops speaking, stops moving. Sam stops playing. Two close-ups reveal Ilsa and Rick seeing each other. Rick isn't breathing at all. It's a wallop, a shock. For a long moment he just looks at her and you can tell what he is thinking. Sam prepares to move the piano away.

Renault and Laszlo are approaching the table from the bar.

RENAULT

to Ilsa
Well, you were asking about Rick and here he is. Mademoiselle, may I present...

RICK

Hello, Ilsa.

ILSA

Hello, Rick.

RENAULT

Oh, you've already met Rick, Mademoiselle?
no answer from either
Well then, perhaps you also...

ILSA

This is Mr. Laszlo.

LASZLO

How do you do?

RICK

How do you do?

LASZLO

One hears a great deal about Rick in Casablanca.

RICK

looks back at him
And about Victor Laszlo everywhere.

LASZLO

Won't you join us for a drink?

RENAULT

laughing
Oh, no, Rick never...

RICK

Thanks. I will.

RENAULT

Well! A precedent is being broken. Er, Emil!

LASZLO

he is making conversation
This is a very interesting cafe. I congratulate you.

RICK

And I congratulate you.

LASZLO

What for?

RICK

Your work.

LASZLO

Thank you. I try.

RICK

We all try. You succeed.

RENAULT

I can't get over you two. She was asking about you earlier, Rick, in a way that made me extremely jealous.

ILSA

to Rick
I wasn't sure you were the same. Let's see, the last time we met...

RICK

It was "La Belle Aurore."

ILSA

How nice. You remembered. But of course, that was the day the Germans marched into Paris.

RICK

Not an easy day to forget.

ILSA

No.

RICK

I remember every detail. The Germans wore gray, you wore blue.

ILSA

Yes. I put that dress away. When the Germans march out, I'll wear it again.

RENAULT

Ricky, you're becoming quite human. I suppose we have to thank you for that, Mademoiselle.

LASZLO

Ilsa, I don't wish to be the one to say it, but it's late.

RENAULT

glancing at his wristwatch
So it is. And we have a curfew here in Casablanca. It would never do for the Chief of Police to be found drinking after hours and have to fine himself.

Rick and Ilsa look at each other.

LASZLO

signaling the waiter
I hope we didn't overstay our welcome.

RICK

Not at all.

WAITER

to Laszlo
Your check, sir.

RICK

takes check
Oh, it's my party.

RENAULT

Another precedent gone. This has been a very interesting evening.
I'll call you a cab. Gasoline rationing, time of night.

Renault leaves.

LASZLO

We'll come again.

RICK

Anytime.

ILSA

Say goodnight to Sam for me.

RICK

I will.

ILSA

There's still nobody in the world who can play ''As Time Goes By''
like Sam.

RICK

He hasn't played it in a long time.

A pause. Ilsa smiles.

ILSA

Goodnight.

LASZLO

Goodnight.

RICK

Goodnight.

Rick and Laszlo nod goodnight to each other. Laszlo and Ilsa start to the door, as Rick sits down again and stares off in their direction.

Ilsa and Laszlo are outside the cafe.

LASZLO

A very puzzling fellow, this Rick. What sort is he?

Ilsa doesn't look at him.

ILSA

Oh, I really can't say, though I saw him quite often in Paris.

They join Renault at the curb.

RENAULT

Tomorrow at ten at the Prefect's office.

LASZLO

We'll be there.

RENAULT

Goodnight.

ILSA

Goodnight.

LASZLO

Goodnight.

They get into the waiting cab, leaving Renault on the curb, smoking and looking bemused.

The cafe sign is just being turned off. The doorway is now illuminated only as the revolving beacon from the airport strikes it.

Inside the cafe, the customers have all gone. The house lights are out. Rick sits at a table. There is a glass of bourbon on the table directly in front of him, and another glass empty on the table before an empty chair. Near at hand is a bottle. Rick just sits. His face is entirely expressionless. The beacon light from the airport sweeps around the room creating a mood of unreality. Sam comes in. He stands hesitantly before Rick.

SAM

Boss.
no answer, as Rick drinks
Boss!

RICK

Yeah?

SAM

Boss, ain't you going to bed?

RICK

filling his glass
Not right now.

Sam realizes Rick is in a grim mood.

SAM

lightly, trying to kid Rick out of it
Ain't you planning on going to bed in the near future?

RICK

No.

SAM

You ever going to bed?

RICK

No.

SAM

still trying
Well, I ain't sleepy either.

RICK

Good. Then have a drink.

SAM

No. Not me, boss.

RICK

Then don't have a drink.

SAM

Boss, let's get out of here.

RICK

emphatically
No, sir. I'm waiting for a lady.

SAM

earnestly
Please, boss, let's go. Ain't nothing but trouble for you here.

RICK

She's coming back. I know she's coming back.

SAM

We'll take the car and drive all night. We'll get drunk. We'll go fishing and stay away until she's gone.

RICK

Shut up and go home, will you?

SAM

stubbornly
No, sir. I'm staying right here.

Sam sits down at the piano and starts to play softly.

RICK

really drunk now
They grab Ugarte and she walks in. Well, that's the way it goes. One in, one out.

pause as he thinks of something
Sam?

SAM

still playing

Yeah, boss?

RICK

Sam, if it's December 1941 in Casablanca, what time is it in New York?

SAM

Uh, my watch stopped.

RICK

drunken nostalgia
I bet they're asleep in New York. I'll bet they're asleep all over America.
pounds the table suddenly
Of all the gin joints in all the towns in all the world, she walks into mine!
irritably, to Sam
What's that you're playing?

SAM

who has been improvising
Just a little something of my own.

RICK

Well, stop it. You know what I want to hear.

SAM

No, I don't.

RICK

You played it for her and you can play it for me.

SAM

Well, I don't think I can remember it.

RICK

If she can stand it, I can. Play it!

SAM

Yes, boss.

Sam starts to play "As Time Goes By."
The camera closes in on Rick. From his expression we know that
he is thinking of the past. Slowly the sounds of an orchestra join
into Sam's playing as the scene dissolves.

It is Paris in spring. A shot of the Arc de Triomphe is followed by
one of Rick driving a small, open car slowly along the boulevard.
Close behind him, with her arm linked in his, sits Ilsa.

On an excursion boat on the Seine. At the rail of the boat stand Rick
and Ilsa. They are transported by each other. Ilsa laughs.

Inside Rick's Paris apartment, Ilsa fixes flowers at the window. Rick
opens champagne. Ilsa joins him.

RICK

Who are you really? And what were you before? What did you do
and what did you think? Huh?

ILSA

We said "no questions."

RICK

Here's looking at you, kid.

They drink.

Inside a swank Paris cafe, Rick and Ilsa dance.

Inside Ilsa's Paris apartment.

ILSA

A franc for your thoughts.

RICK

In America they'd bring only a penny. I guess that's about all they're worth.

ILSA

I'm willing to be overcharged. Tell me.

RICK

I was wondering.

ILSA

Yes?

RICK

Why I'm so lucky. Why I should find you waiting for me to come along.

ILSA

Why there is no other man in my life?

RICK

Uh huh.

ILSA

That's easy. There was. He's dead.

RICK

Well, only one answer can take care of all our questions.

ILSA

Well, only one question can take care of all our questions.
She kisses him.

Newsreel footage of the German occupation of France.

A man sells newspapers to people crowded around him. There is much excitement. Rick and Ilsa, sitting in a cafe, buy the newspaper and read it. Nearby, a group of frightened French people cluster around a loudspeaker wagon. A harsh voice is barking out the tragic news of the Nazi push toward Paris.

RICK

Nothing can stop them now. Wednesday, Thursday at the latest, they'll be in Paris.

ILSA

frightened
Richard, they'll find out your record. It won't be safe for you here.

RICK

smiles
I'm on their blacklist already, their roll of honor.

A small cafe in the Montmartre. A shadow on the floor reflects the cafe sign ''La Belle Aurore.'' Rick is at the bar getting glasses and a bottle of champagne. He walks over to Ilsa and Sam at the piano. Sam is playing ''As Time Goes By.'' Ilsa's attitude, as she listens, is very distraught. There is evidently something on her mind, and it isn't all concerned with the war. Rick pours the champagne. His manner is wry, but not the bitter wryness we have seen in Casablanca.

RICK

Henri wants us to finish this bottle and then three more. He says he'll water his garden with champagne before he'll let the Germans drink any of it.

SAM

looking at his glass
This sort of takes the sting out of being occupied, doesn't it, Mr. Richard?

RICK

You said it!
to Ilsa
Here's looking at you, kid.
A loudspeaker is heard in the street. Rick and Ilsa look at each other, then hurry to the window. The loudspeaker is blaring in German.

RICK

My German's a little rusty.

ILSA

sadly
It's the Gestapo. They say they expect to be in Paris tomorrow. They are telling us how to act when they come marching in.
smiling faintly
With the whole world crumbling, we pick this time to fall in love.

RICK

Yeah. It's pretty bad timing.
looks at her
Where were you, say, ten years ago?

ILSA

trying to cheer up
Ten years ago? Let's see...
thinks
Yes. I was having a brace put on my teeth. Where were you?

RICK

Looking for a job.

Pause. Ilsa looks at him tenderly. Rick takes her in his arms, and kisses her hungrily. While they are locked in an embrace the dull boom of cannons is heard. Rick and Ilsa separate.

ILSA

frightened, but trying not to show it
Was that cannon fire, or is it my heart pounding?

RICK

grimly
Ah, that's the new German 77. And judging by the sound, only about thirty-five miles away.

another booming is heard
And getting closer every minute. Here. Drink up. We'll never finish the other three.

SAM

The Germans'll be here pretty soon now, and they'll come looking for you. And don't forget there's a price on your head.
Ilsa reacts to this worriedly.

RICK

dryly
I left a note in my apartment. They'll know where to find me.

Ilsa looks at Rick

ILSA

Strange. I know so very little about you.

RICK

I know very little about you; just the fact that you had your teeth straightened.

ILSA

But be serious, darling. You are in danger and you must leave Paris.

RICK

No, no, no, no. *We* must leave.

ILSA

worried
Yes, of course, we.

RICK

The train for Marseilles leaves at five o'clock. I'll pick you up at your hotel at four-thirty.

ILSA

quickly
No, no. Not at my hotel. I er, I have things to do in the city before I leave. I'll meet you at the station, huh?

RICK

All right. At a quarter to five.
a thought strikes him
Say, why don't we get married in Marseilles?

ILSA

evasively
That's too far ahead to plan.

RICK

happy, excited at the thought of leaving with Ilsa
Yes, I guess it is a little too far ahead. Well, let's see. What about the engineer? Why can't he marry us on the train?

ILSA

laughing nervously
Oh, darling!
Suddenly Ilsa starts to cry softly.

RICK

Well, why not? The captain on a ship can. It doesn't seem fair that...Hey, hey, what's wrong, kid?

ILSA

controlling herself
I love you so much, and I hate this war so much.
stops, looks at Rick
Oh, it's a crazy world. Anything can happen. If you shouldn't get away, I mean, if, if something should keep up apart, wherever they put you and wherever I'll be, I want you to know that I...
She can't go on. She lifts her face to his. He kisses her gently.

ILSA

Kiss me. Kiss me as if it were the last time.

He looks into her eyes, then kisses her as though it were the last time. Her hand falls to the table, knocking over a glass. In the Gare de Lyon, there is a hectic, fevered excitement evident in the faces we pass. This is the last train from Paris! Rick appears in the crowd. He stops in front of the clock and puts his suitcase down. He glances at his watch. It is two minutes before train time. Rain is pouring over his head and shoulders, but he seems not to notice. He checks his watch again. Suddenly Sam appears.

RICK

Where is she? Have you seen her?

SAM

No, Mr. Richard. I can't find her. She checked out of the hotel. But this note came just after you left.
Sam pulls an envelope from his pocket. Rick grabs it, opens it, and stares down at the letter, which reads:
''Richard:
I cannot go with you or ever see you again. You must not ask why. Just believe that I love you. Go, my darling, and God bless you. Ilsa''

Richard,

I cannot go with you or ever see you again. You must not ask why. Just believe that I love you. So my darling and God bless you.

The raindrops pour down the letter, smudging the writing. A whistle blows.

SAM

frantically
That's the last call, Mr. Richard, do you hear me? Come on, Mr. Richard. Let's get out of here. Come on, Mr. Richard, come on.

Sam pulls a stunned, reluctant Rick to the train. He looks back. The train starts to move just as he boards. From the steps, he looks off into the distance, then crumbles the letter and tosses it away as the steam from the engine clouds over the scene.

When the haze clears, there is a close-up of a glass on the table in the cafe. Rick's hand reaches for it and knocks it over. The camera pans to Rick's face. He is drunk. Sam walks over to the table to pick up the glass and a fallen chair. Just then the door opens and Ilsa is there. Rick is staring at the doorway. Ilsa lingers a moment, then moves over to the table.

ILSA

Rick, I have to talk to you.
Her manner is a little uncertain, a little tentative, but with a quiet determination beneath it.

RICK

Oh. I saved my first drink to have with you. Here.

ILSA

No. No, Rick. Not tonight.

RICK

Especially tonight.

She sits down in the chair before the empty glass. Her eyes are searching his face, but there is no expression on it except a cold and impassive one. Reaching for the bottle, he pours himself another drink.

ILSA

Please.

RICK

Why did you have to come to Casablanca? There are other places.

ILSA

I wouldn't have come if I had known that you were here. Believe me, Rick, it's true. I didn't know.

RICK

It's funny about your voice, how it hasn't changed. I can still hear it. "Richard dear, I'll go with you anyplace. We'll get on a train together and never stop."

ILSA

Please don't. Don't, Rick! I can understand how you feel.

RICK

Huh! You understand how I feel. How long was it we had, honey?

ILSA

I didn't count the days.

RICK

Well, I did. Every one of them. Mostly I remember the last one. A wow finish. A guy standing on a station platform in the rain with

a comical look on his face, because his insides had been kicked out.
He takes a drink.

ILSA

after a pause
Can I tell you a story, Rick?

RICK

Has it got a wow finish?

ILSA

I don't know the finish yet.

RICK

Well, go on, tell it. Maybe one will come to you as you go along.

ILSA

It's about a girl who had just come to Paris from her home in Oslo. At the house of some friends she met a man about whom she'd heard her whole life, a very great and courageous man. He opened up for her a whole beautiful world full of knowledge and thoughts and ideals. Everything she knew or ever became was because of him. And she looked up to him and worshipped him with a feeling she supposed was love.

RICK

Yes, that's very pretty. I heard a story once. As a matter of fact, I've heard a lot of stories in my time. They went along with the sound of a tinny piano playing in the parlor downstairs, "Mister, I met a man once when I was a kid," it'd always begin.
pause
Huh. I guess neither one of our stories was very funny. Tell me,

127

who was it you left me for? Was it Laszlo, or were there others in between? Or aren't you the kind that tells?

Ilsa, shuddering, gets up and leaves. Rick's head slumps over the table.

The next morning in Renault's office, Strasser is with Renault.

STRASSER

I strongly suspect that Ugarte left the letters of transit with Mr. Blaine. I would suggest you search the cafe immediately and thoroughly.

RENAULT

If Rick has the letters, he's much too smart to let you find them there.

STRASSER

You give him credit for too much cleverness. My impression was that he's just another blundering American.

RENAULT

But we mustn't underestimate American blundering.
innocently
I was with them when they "blundered" into Berlin in 1918.

Strasser looks at him.

STRASSER

As to Laszlo, we want him watched twenty-four hours a day.

RENAULT

reassuringly
It may interest you to know that at this very moment he is on his way here.

Laszlo and Ilsa make their way through the jam in the lobby of the Prefecture. Jan and Annina are there, talking to an officer.

OFFICER

to Jan and Annina
There's nothing we can do.

Laszlo and Ilsa enter Renault's office. He bows to them both.

RENAULT

I am delighted to see you both. Did you have a good night's rest?

LASZLO

I slept very well.

RENAULT

That's strange. Nobody is supposed to sleep well in Casablanca.

LASZLO

briefly
May we proceed with the business?

RENAULT

With pleasure. Won't you sit down?

LASZLO

Thank you.

STRASSER

now as cold as Laszlo.
Very well, Herr Laszlo, we will not mince words. You are an escaped prisoner of the Reich. So far you have been fortunate enough in

eluding us. You have reached Casablanca. It is my duty to see that you stay in Casablanca.

LASZLO

Whether or not you succeed is, of course, problematical.

STRASSER

Not at all. Captain Renault's signature is necessary on every exit visa.
turns to Renault
Captain, would you think it is possible that Herr Laszlo will receive a visa?

RENAULT

I am afraid not. My regrets, M'sieur.

LASZLO

Well, perhaps I shall like it in Casablanca.

STRASSER

And Mademoiselle?

ILSA

You needn't be concerned about me.

LASZLO

prepares to rise
Is that all you wish to tell us?

STRASSER

Don't be in such a hurry. You have all the time in the world. You may be in Casablanca indefinitely...

suddenly leans forward, speaks intently
...or you may leave for Lisbon tomorrow, on one condition.

LASZLO

And that is?

STRASSER

You know the leaders of the underground movement in Paris, in Prague, in Brussels, in Amsterdam, in Oslo, in Belgrade, in Athens.

LASZLO

Even in Berlin.

STRASSER

Yes, even in Berlin. If you will furnish me with their names and their exact whereabouts, you will have your visa in the morning.

RENAULT

tongue in cheek again
And the honor of having served the Third Reich!

LASZLO

I was in a German concentration camp for a year. That's honor enough for a lifetime.

STRASSER

You will give us the names?

LASZLO

If I didn't give them to you in a concentration camp where you had more "persuasive methods" at your disposal, I certainly won't give them to you now.

the passionate conviction in his voice now revealing the crusader
And what if you track down these men and kill them? What if you murdered all of us? From every corner of Europe, hundreds, thousands, would rise to take our places. Even Nazis can't kill that fast.

STRASSER

Herr Laszlo, you have a reputation for eloquence which I can now understand. But in one respect you are mistaken. You said the enemies of the Reich could all be replaced, but there is one exception. No one could take your place in the event anything unfortunate should occur to you while you were trying to escape.

LASZLO

You won't dare to interfere with me here. This is still unoccupied France. Any violation of neutrality would reflect on Captain Renault.

RENAULT

M'sieur, insofar as it is in my power...

LASZLO

Thank you.

RENAULT

By the way, M'sieur, last night you evinced an interest in Signor Ugarte.

LASZLO

Yes.

RENAULT

I believe you have a message for him?

LASZLO

Nothing important, but may I speak to him now?

STRASSER

wryly
You would find the conversation a trifle one-sided. Signor Ugarte
is dead.

*Close-ups of Ilsa, then Laszlo, reveal their disappointment. Strasser
observes.*

ILSA

Oh.

RENAULT

holding the report
I am making out the report now. We haven't quite decided whether
he committed suicide or died trying to escape.

LASZLO

Are you quite finished with us?

STRASSER

For the time being.

LASZLO

Good day.

*As Ilsa and Laszlo leave, an officer comes in. When the door has
closed on Ilsa and Laszlo, Renault speaks to Strasser.*

RENAULT

Undoubtedly their next step will be to the black market.

OFFICER

Excuse me, Captain. Another visa problem has come up.

RENAULT

happily, as he looks at himself in the mirror
Show her in.

OFFICER

Yes, sir.

The black market is a cluttered Arab street of bazaars, shops and stalls. All kinds and races of people are milling about the merchandise which native dealers have on outdoor display. Both men and women are dressed in tropical clothes. The canopies over the stalls give them some protection from the scorching sun. On the surface, the atmosphere is merely languid, but there is the sinister undercurrent of illicit trade.

A Frenchman and a native are talking together in low tones.

NATIVE

I'm sorry, M'sieur, we would have to handle the police. This is a job for Signor Ferrari.

MAN

Ferrari?

NATIVE

It can be most helpful to know Signor Ferrari. He's pretty near got a monopoly on the black market here. You will find him over there at the Blue Parrot.

MAN

Thanks.

Outside the cafe, a blue parrot sits on a perch. Inside, the cafe is much less pretentious than Rick's, but well populated. Rick enters and walks through the cafe toward Ferrari's office just as Ferrari is emerging with Jan and Annina, who look very downhearted.

FERRARI

There, don't be too downhearted. Perhaps you can come to terms with Captain Renault.

JAN

Thank you very much, Signor.

He leads Annina away. Rick is behind Ferrari and calls out to him.

RICK

Hello, Ferrari.

Signor Ferrari turns around, pleased to see Rick.

FERRARI

Ah, good morning, Rick.

RICK

I see the bus is in. I'll take my shipment with me.

FERRARI

No hurry. I'll have it sent over. Have a drink with me.

RICK

I never drink in the morning. And every time you send my shipment over, it's always just a little bit short.

FERRARI

chuckling
Carrying charges, my boy, carrying charges. Here, sit down. There's something I want to talk over with you, anyhow.
hailing a waiter
The bourbon.
to Rick, sighing deeply
The news about Ugarte upset me very much.

RICK

You're a fat hypocrite. You don't feel any sorrier for Ugarte than I do.

FERRARI

eyes Rick closely
Of course not. What upsets me is the fact that Ugarte is dead and no one knows where those letters of transit are.

RICK

dead-pan
Practically no one.

FERRARI

If I could lay my hands on those letters, I could make a fortune.

RICK

So could I. And I'm a poor businessman.

FERRARI

I have a proposition for whoever has those letters. I will handle the entire transaction, get rid of the letters, take all the risk, for a small percentage.

RICK

And the carrying charges?

FERRARI

smiling
Naturally there will be a few incidental expenses.
looking at Rick squarely
That is the proposition I have for whoever has those letters.

RICK

dryly
I'll tell him when he comes in.

FERRARI

Rick, I'll put my cards on the table. I think you know where those letters are.

RICK

Well, you're in good company. Renault and Strasser probably think so, too.
looks out of the window to see Laszlo walking toward the cafe leaving Ilsa at the linen bazaar
That's why I came over here to give them a chance to ransack my place.

FERRARI

Rick, don't be a fool. Take me into your confidence. You need a partner.

Rick isn't listening to him. He is looking through the open window in the direction of the linen bazaar.

RICK

getting up
Excuse me, I'll be getting back.

Laszlo reaches the entrance to the cafe as Rick is coming out. He stops and addresses Rick politely.

LASZLO

Good morning.

RICK

Signor Ferrari is the fat gent at the table.

As he exits, Laszlo looks after him with a puzzled expression.

At the linen stall, Ilsa is examining a tablecloth which an Arab vendor is endeavoring to sell. He is holding a sign which reads ''700 francs.''

ARAB

You will not find a treasure like this in all Morocco, Mademoiselle. Only seven hundred francs.

Rick walks up behind Ilsa.

RICK

You're being cheated.

She looks briefly at Rick, then turns away. Her manner is politely formal.

ILSA

It doesn't matter, thank you.

ARAB

Ah, the lady is a friend of Rick's? For friends of Rick we have a small discount. Did I say seven hundred francs? You can have it for two hundred.

Reaching under the counter, he takes out a sign reading, ''200 francs'' and replaces the other sign with it.

RICK

I'm sorry I was in no condition to receive you when you called on me last night.

ILSA

It doesn't matter.

ARAB

Ah, for *special* friends of Rick's we have a *special* discount. One hundred francs.

He replaces the second sign with a third which reads, ''100 francs.''

RICK

Your story had me a little confused. Or maybe it was the bourbon.

ARAB

I have some tablecloths, some napkins...

ILSA

Thank you. I'm really not interested.

ARAB

Please, one minute. Wait!
hurriedly exits

Ilsa pretends to examine the goods on the counter.

RICK

Why did you come back? To tell me why you ran out on me at the railway station?

ILSA

quietly
Yes.

RICK

Well, you can tell me now. I'm reasonably sober.

ILSA

I don't think I will, Rick.

RICK

Why not? After all, I got stuck with a railway ticket. I think I'm entitled to know.

ILSA

slowly

Last night I saw what has happened to you. The Rick I knew in Paris,
I could tell him. He'd understand. But the one who looked at me
with such hatred...well, I'll be leaving Casablanca soon and we'll
never see each other again.

now looking at him

We knew very little about each other when we were in love in Paris.
If we leave it that way, maybe we'll remember those days and not
Casablanca, not last night.

RICK

his voice low but intense

Did you run out on me because you couldn't take it? Because you
knew what it would be like, hiding from the police, running away
all the time?

ILSA

You can believe that if you want to.

RICK

Well, I'm not running away any more. I'm settled now, above a
saloon, it's true, but...

ironically

Walk up a flight. I'll be expecting you.

Ilsa turns her head away.

RICK

All the same, someday you'll lie to Laszlo. You'll be there!

ILSA

No, Rick, no. You see, Victor Laszlo is my husband.

Rick stares at her.

ILSA

And was, even when I knew you in Paris.

She walks away into the cafe as Rick stares after her.

Inside, Ilsa sits with Laszlo and Ferrari.

FERRARI

I was just telling M'sieur Laszlo that, unfortunately, I am not able to help him.

ILSA

troubled
Oh.

LASZLO

You see, my dear, the word has gone around.

FERRARI

to Ilsa
As leader of all illegal activities in Casablanca, I am an influential and respected man. It would not be worth my life to do anything for M'sieur Laszlo. You, however, are a different matter.

LASZLO

Signor Ferrari thinks it might just be possible to get an exit visa for you.

ILSA

You mean for me to go on alone?

FERRARI

And *only* alone.

LASZLO

I will stay here and keep on trying. I'm sure in a little while...

FERRARI

We might as well be frank, M'sieur. It will take a miracle to get you out of Casablanca. And the Germans have outlawed miracles.

ILSA

to Ferrari
We are only interested in two visas, Signor.

LASZLO

Please, Ilsa, don't be hasty.

ILSA

firmly
No, Victor, no.

FERRARI

You two will want to discuss this. Excuse me. I'll be at the bar.

Ferrari gets to his feet and walks away.

LASZLO

No, Ilsa, I won't let you stay here. You must get to America. And believe me, somehow I will get out and join you.

ILSA

But, Victor, if the situation were different, if I had to stay and there were only a visa for one, would you take it?

Laszlo hesitates.

LASZLO

not very convincingly
Yes, I would.

Ilsa smiles faintly.

ILSA

Yes, I see. When I had trouble getting out of Lille, why didn't you leave me there? And when I was sick in Marseilles and held you up for two weeks and you were in danger every minute of the time, why didn't you leave me then?

LASZLO

with a wry smile
I meant to, but something always held me up.
reaches over, puts his hand over hers
I love you very much, Ilsa.

ILSA

smiling
Your secret will be safe with me. Ferrari is waiting for our answer.

At the bar Ferrari is talking to a waiter.

FERRARI

Not more than fifty francs though.

Ilsa and Laszlo walk up to him.

LASZLO

We've decided, Signor Ferrari. For the present we'll go on looking for two exit visas. Thank you very much.

FERRARI

Well, good luck. But be careful.
a flick of his eyes in the direction of the bazaar
You know you're being shadowed?

LASZLO

glancing in the direction of the bazaar
Of course. It becomes an instinct.

FERRARI

shrewdly looking at Ilsa
I observe that you in one respect are a very fortunate man, M'sieur. I am moved to make one more suggestion, why, I do not know, because it cannot possibly profit me, but, have you heard about Signor Ugarte and the letters of transit?

LASZLO

Yes, something.

FERRARI

Those letters were not found on Ugarte when they arrested him.

LASZLO

after a moment's pause
Do you know where they are?

FERRARI

Not for sure, M'sieur, but I will venture to guess that Ugarte left those letters with M'sieur Rick.

Ilsa's face darkens. Laszlo quietly observes.

LASZLO

Rick?

FERRARI

He is a difficult customer, that Rick. One never knows what he'll do or why. But it is worth a chance.

LASZLO

Thank you very much. Good day.

ILSA

Goodbye, thank you for your coffee, Signor. I shall miss that when we leave Casablanca.

FERRARI

bows
It was gracious of you to share it with me. Good day, Mademoiselle, M'sieur

LASZLO

Good day.

As Ilsa and Laszlo leave the cafe, Ferrari nonchalantly swats a fly on a table.

Outside Rick's cafe, the sign is lit up and the sounds of music filter out into the air. Inside at the bar, the dark European has found another tourist.

DARK EUROPEAN

Here's to you, sir.

TOURIST

Er, good luck, yes.

DARK EUROPEAN

I'd better be going.

TOURIST

Er, my check, please.

DARK EUROPEAN

I have to warn you, sir. I beseech you...

The tourist laughs nervously. The dark European picks his pocket.

DARK EUROPEAN

This is a dangerous place, full of vultures. Vultures everywhere!
Thanks for everything.

TOURIST

laughing
Er, goodbye, sir.

DARK EUROPEAN

It has been a pleasure to meet you.
dashing off and colliding with Carl
Oh, I'm sorry.

As the dark European hurries away, Carl checks all his pockets to make sure nothing is missing.

Sam and Corina finish their number. Strasser and his crowd enter the cafe and pass Rick's table. Carl brings Rick a bottle and glass.

CARL

M'sieur Rick, you are getting to be your best customer.

Carl exits; Renault comes up to Rick.

RENAULT

Well, Ricky. I'm very pleased with you. Now you're beginning to live like a Frenchman.

RICK

That was some going-over your men gave my place this afternoon. We just barely got cleaned up in time to open.

RENAULT

Well, I told Strasser he wouldn't find the letters here. But I told my men to be especially destructive. You know how that impresses Germans? Rick, have you got these letters of transit?

RICK

steadily
Louis, are you pro-Vichy or Free French?

RENAULT

promptly
Serves me right for asking a direct question. The subject is closed.

RICK

Well, it looks like you're a little late.

RENAULT

Huh?

Rick is gazing at Yvonne and a German officer approaching the bar.

RICK

So Yvonne's gone over to the enemy.

RENAULT

Who knows? In her own way she may constitute an entire second front.
gets up
I think it's time for me to flatter Major Strasser a little. I'll see you later, Rick.
he strolls away.

At the bar, Yvonne and the German officer place their order.

YVONNE

Sacha!

GERMAN OFFICER

French seventy-fives.

YVONNE

somewhat tight already
Put up a whole row of them, Sacha...
indicating on the bar with her hand
...starting here and ending here.

GERMAN OFFICER

cutting in
We will begin with two.

A French officer at the bar makes a remark to Yvonne.

FRENCH OFFICER

in French
Say, you, you are not French to go with a German like this!

YVONNE

in French
What are you butting in for?

FRENCH OFFICER

in French
I am butting in...

YVONNE

breaking in, in French
It's none of your business!

GERMAN OFFICER

in French
No, no, no, no! One minute!
in English
What did you say? Would you kindly repeat it?

FRENCH OFFICER

What I said is none of your business!

GERMAN OFFICER

I will make it my business!

They begin to fight.

YVONNE

in French
Stop! I beg of you! I beg of you, stop!

There are exclamations from people nearby. German officers at a table rise, ready to join in. Rick walks up and separates the two men.

RICK

to the German
I don't like disturbances in my place. Either lay off politics or get out.

FRENCH OFFICER

in French
Dirty Boche. Someday we'll have our revenge!

At Strasser's table, Renault, Strasser and the others sit down again.

STRASSER

You see, Captain, the situation is not as much under control as you believe.

RENAULT

My dear Major, we are trying to cooperate with your government, but we cannot regulate the feelings of our people.

STRASSER

eyes him closely

Captain Renault, are you entirely certain which side you're on?

RENAULT

I have no conviction, if that's what you mean. I blow with the wind, and the prevailing wind happens to be from Vichy.

STRASSER

And if it should change?

RENAULT

smiles
Surely the Reich doesn't admit that possibility?

STRASSER

We are concerned about more than Casablanca. We know that every French province in Africa is honeycombed with traitors waiting for their chance, waiting, perhaps, for a leader.

RENAULT

casually
A leader, like Laszlo?

STRASSER

Uh, huh. I have been thinking. It is too dangerous if we let him go. It may be too dangerous if we let him stay.

RENAULT

thoughtfully
I see what you mean.

Carl approaches the Leuchtags' table with a bottle. They are a middle-aged couple.

CARL

in German
I brought you the finest brandy. Only the employees drink it here.

MR. LEUCHTAG

Thank you, Carl.

CARL

as he pours
For Mrs. Leuchtag.

MRS. LEUCHTAG

Thank you, Carl.

CARL

For Mr. Leuchtag.

MR. LEUCHTAG

Carl, sit down. Have a brandy with us.

MRS. LEUCHTAG

beaming with happiness
To celebrate our leaving for America tomorrow.

CARL

sitting
Thank you very much. I thought you would ask me, so I brought
the good brandy and a third glass.

MRS. LEUCHTAG

At last the day has came.

MR. LEUCHTAG

Frau Leuchtag and I are speaking nothing but English now.

MRS. LEUCHTAG

So we should feel at home ven ve get to America.

CARL

A very nice idea.

MR. LEUCHTAG

raising his glass
To America.

Mrs. Leuchtag and Carl repeat ''To America.'' They clink glasses and drink.

MR. LEUCHTAG

Liebchen, uh, sweetness heart, what watch?

MRS. LEUCHTAG

glancing at her wristwatch
Ten watch.

MR. LEUCHTAG

surprised
Such much?

CARL

Er, you will get along beautifully in America, huh.

Coming from the gambling room, Annina meets Renault in the hallway.

RENAULT

How's lady luck treating you? Aw, too bad. You'll find him over there.

Annina sees Rick and goes to his table.

ANNINA

M'sieur Rick?

RICK

Yes?

ANNINA

Could I speak to you for just a moment, please?

Rick looks at her.

RICK

How did you get in here? You're under age.

ANNINA

I came with Captain Renault.

RICK

cynically
I should have known.

ANNINA

My husband is with me, too.

RICK

He is? Well, Captain Renault's getting broadminded. Sit down. Will you have a drink?

Annina shakes her head.

RICK

No, of course not. Do you mind if I do?

ANNINA

No.
nervously, as Rick pours himself a drink
M'sieur Rick, what kind of man is Captain Renault?

RICK

Oh, he's just like any other man, only more so.

ANNINA

No, I mean, is he trustworthy? Is his word...

RICK

Now, just a minute. Who told you to ask me that?

ANNINA

He did. Captain Renault did.

RICK

I thought so. Where's your husband?

ANNINA

At the roulette table, trying to win enough for our exit visa. Of course, he's losing.

Rick looks at her closely.

RICK

How long have you been married?

ANNINA

simply
Eight weeks. We come from Bulgaria. Oh, things are very bad there, M'sieur. A devil has the people by the throat. So Jan and I, we, we do not want our children to grow up in such a country.

RICK

wearily
So you decided to go to America.

ANNINA

Yes, but we have not much money, and travelling is so expensive and difficult. It was much more than we thought to get here. And then Captain Renault sees us and he is so kind. He wants to help us.

RICK

Yes, I'll bet.

ANNINA

He tells me he can give us an exit visa, but we have no money.

RICK

Does he know that?

ANNINA

Oh, yes.

RICK

And he is still willing to give you a visa?

ANNINA

Yes, M'sieur.

RICK

And you want to know...

ANNINA

Will he keep his word?

RICK

looking at his drink
He always has.

There is a silence. Annina is very disturbed.

ANNINA

Oh, M'sieur, you are a man. If someone loved you very much, so that your happiness was the only thing that she wanted in the whole world, but she did a bad thing to make certain of it, could you forgive her?

RICK

staring off into space
Nobody ever loved me that much.

ANNINA

And he never knew, and the girl kept this bad thing locked in her heart? That would be all right, wouldn't it?

RICK

harshly
You want my advice?

ANNINA

Oh, yes, please.

RICK

Go back to Bulgaria.

ANNINA

Oh, but if you knew what it means to us to leave Europe, to get to America! Oh, but if Jan should find out! He is such a boy. In many ways I am so much older than he is.

RICK

Yes, well, everybody in Casablanca has problems. Yours may work out. You'll excuse me.

Rick gets up and leaves Annina at the table.

ANNINA

tonelessly
Thank you, M'sieur.

She remains seated.

Rick is checking the reservation list at the desk when he sees Ilsa and Laszlo enter the cafe. He comes up to them.

RICK

Good evening.

LASZLO

Good evening. You see, here we are again.

RICK

I take that as a great compliment to Sam.
to Ilsa
I suppose he means to you Paris of, well, happier days.

ILSA

quietly
He does. Could we have a table close to him?

LASZLO

who has been looking around
And as far from Major Strasser as possible.

RICK

Well, the geography might be a little difficult to arrange.
snaps his fingers for the headwaiter
Paul! Table thirty!

HEADWAITER

to Ilsa and Laszlo
Yes, sir. Right this way, if you please.

RICK

to Ilsa
I'll have Sam play ''As Time Goes By.'' I believe that's your favorite tune.

ILSA

smiling
Thank you.

Rick walks over to Sam and whispers something to him. Sam stops what he is playing and begins "As Time Goes By," shaking his head. Laszlo orders.

LASZLO

Two cognacs, please.

Rick goes to the gambling room. Inside, at the roulette table, Jan's eyes are tragic. He has only three chips left. He seems bewildered. As Rick comes up, the croupier is speaking to Jan:

CROUPIER

Do you wish to place another bet, sir?

JAN

No, no, I guess not.

Rick stands behind Jan.

RICK

to Jan, dead-pan
Have you tried twenty-two tonight? I said, twenty-two.

Jan looks at Rick, then at the chips in his hand. A pause. He puts the chips on twenty-two.

Rick and the croupier exchange looks. The croupier understands what Rick wants him to do. He spins the wheel. In the background, Carl is looking at the wheel, fascinated. The wheel stops spinning.

CROUPIER

calling out in French
Twenty-two, black, twenty-two.

The croupier pushes a pile of chips onto the number. Jan reaches for it. Renault, at a nearby table, takes notice of what is happening.

RICK

not even looking at Jan
Leave it there.

Jan hesitates, then withdraws his hands. In the background, Carl draws a little closer. The wheel spins. Nobody speaks while it spins. It stops.

CROUPIER

Twenty-two, black.

In the background, Carl gasps. The croupier shoves a pile of chips toward Jan. Renault looks miffed.

RICK

to Jan
Cash it in and don't come back.

A customer complains to Carl.

CUSTOMER

Say, you sure this place is honest?

CARL

fervently
Honest! As honest as the day is long!

While Jan and Annina cash their chips, Rick speaks to the croupier.

RICK

How we doing tonight?

CROUPIER

dryly
Well, a couple of thousand less than I thought there would be.

Rick smiles slightly and exits toward the bar. Annina runs up to him and hugs him.

ANNINA

M'sieur Rick, I...

RICK

He's just a lucky guy.

CARL

solicitously
M'sieur Rick, may I get you a cup of coffee?

RICK

No thanks, Carl.

CARL

M'sieur Rick!

Renault seeing that Jan has won, gets up from his table to follow Rick. Jan and Annina stop him on the way.

JAN

Captain Renault, may I...?

RENAULT

Oh, not here, please. Come to my office in the morning. We'll do everything business-like.

JAN

We'll be there at six.

RENAULT

I'll be there at ten.
smiling insincerely
I am very happy for both of you. Still, it's strange that you won.
he looks off and sees Rick
Well, maybe not so strange. I'll see you in the morning.

ANNINA

Thank you so much, Captain Renault.

At the bar, Carl whispers in Sacha's ear. Sacha says "No!"
He runs to Rick.

SACHA

Boss, you've done a beautiful thing.

He kisses Rick on both cheeks.

RICK

Go away, you crazy Russian!

Carl pours a brandy for Rick. Pretending not to do so, Rick is glancing in Ilsa's direction. Renault comes up to him.

RENAULT

As I suspected, you're a rank sentimentalist.

RICK

Yeah? Why?

RENAULT

chidingly
Why do you interfere with my little romances?

RICK

Put it down as a gesture to love.

RENAULT

good-naturedly
Well, I forgive you this time. But I'll be in tomorrow night with a breathtaking blonde, and it will make me very happy if she loses. Uh huh!

He smiles and walks off toward the gambling room. Laszlo comes up to Rick.

LASZLO

M'sieur Blaine, I wonder if I could talk to you?

RICK

Go ahead.

LASZLO

Well, isn't there some other place? It's rather confidential, what I have to say.

RICK

My office.

LASZLO

Right.

In the office.

LASZLO

You must know it's very important I get out of Casablanca.
simply
It's my privilege to be one of the leaders of a great movement. You know what I have been doing. You know what it means to the work, to the lives of thousands and thousands of people that I be free to reach America and continue my work.

RICK

I'm not interested in politics. The problems of the world are not in my department. I'm a saloon keeper.

LASZLO

My friends in the underground tell me that you have quite a record. You ran guns to Ethiopia. You fought against the fascists in Spain.

RICK

What of it?

LASZLO

Isn't it strange that you always happened to be fighting on the side of the underdog?

RICK

Yes. I found that a very expensive hobby, too. But then I never was much of a businessman.

LASZLO

Are you enough of a businessman to appreciate an offer of a hundred thousand francs?

RICK

I appreciate it, but I don't accept it.

LASZLO

I'll raise it to two hundred thousand.

RICK

My friend, you could make it a million francs, or three; My answer would still be the same.

LASZLO

There must be some reason why you won't let me have them.

RICK

There is. I suggest that you ask your wife.

Laszlo looks at him, puzzled.

LASZLO

I beg your pardon?

RICK

I said, ask your wife.

LASZLO

My wife!

RICK

Yes.

Rick and Laszlo hear the sound of male voices singing downstairs. From the top of the stairs outside the office Rick sees a group of German officers around the piano singing the ''Wacht am Rhein.'' Rick's expression is dead-pan. Below, at the bar, Renault watches with raised eyebrow. Laszlo has come out of the office. His lips are very tight as he listens to the song. He starts down the steps, passes the table where Ilsa sits, and goes straight to the orchestra. Yvonne, sitting at a table with her German officer, stares down into her drink. Laszlo speaks to the orchestra.

LASZLO

Play the Marseillaise! Play it!

Members of the orchestra glance toward the steps, toward Rick, who nods to them. As they start to play, Laszlo and Carmina sing. Strasser conducts the German singing in an attempt to drown out the competition. People in the cafe begin to sing. Finally Strasser and his officers give up and sit down. The ''Marseillaise'' continues, however, and now Yvonne has jumped up and is singing with tears in her eyes. Ilsa, overcome with emotion, looks proudly at Laszlo who sings with passion. Finally the whole cafe is standing, singing, their faces aglow. The song is finished on a high, triumphant note.

Yvonne's face is exalted. She deliberately faces the alcove where the Germans are watching. She shouts at the top of her lungs.

YVONNE

Vive La France! Vive la democracie!

CROWD

Vive La France! Vive la democracie!

People are clapping and cheering. Several French officers surround Laszlo, offering him a drink. Strasser's looks are not pleasant. He strides across the floor toward Renault who is standing at the bar.

STRASSER

You see what I mean? If Laszlo's presence in a cafe can inspire this unfortunate demonstration, what more will his presence in Casablanca bring on? I advise that this place be shut up at once.

RENAULT

innocently
But everybody's having such a good time.

STRASSER

Yes, much too good a time. The place is to be closed.

RENAULT

But I have no excuse to close it.

STRASSER

snapping
Find one.

Renault thinks a moment, then blows a loud blast on his whistle.
The room grows quiet, all eyes turn toward Renault.

RENAULT

loudly
Everybody is to leave here immediately! This cafe is closed until further notice!

An angry murmur starts among the crowd.

RENAULT

Clear the room at once!

Rick comes quickly up to Renault.

RICK

How can you close me up? On what grounds?

RENAULT

I am shocked, *shocked* to find that gambling is going on in here!

This display of nerve leaves Rick at a loss. The croupier comes out of the gambling room and up to Renault.

CROUPIER

handing Renault a roll of bills
Your winnings, sir.

RENAULT

Oh. Thank you very much.
turns to the crowd again
Everybody out at once!

As the cafe is emptying, Strasser approaches Ilsa. His manner is abrupt but cordial.

STRASSER

Mademoiselle, after this disturbance it is not safe for Laszlo to stay in Casablanca.

ILSA

This morning you implied it was not safe for him to leave Casablanca.

STRASSER

That is also true, except for one destination, to return to occupied France.

ILSA

Occupied France?

STRASSER

Uh huh. Under a safe conduct from me.

ILSA

with intensity
What value is that? You may recall what German guarantees have been worth in the past.

STRASSER

There are only two other alternatives for him.

ILSA

What are they?

STRASSER

It is possible the French authorities will find a reason to put him in the concentration camp here.

ILSA

And the other alternative?

STRASSER

My dear Mademoiselle, perhaps you have already observed that in Casablanca, human life is cheap. Good night, Mademoiselle.

She looks at him, understanding what he means. He bows and exits as Laszlo arrives at the table. They start out of the cafe.

ILSA

What happened with Rick?

LASZLO

We'll discuss it later.

In the hallway of the hotel, Ilsa and Laszlo are walking to their room. They enter. Laszlo switches on the light and walks to the window to draw the shade. Below, across the street, a man can be seen standing under an arch. Laszlo watches him.

LASZLO

as he draws the shade
Our faithful friend is still there.

ILSA

Victor, please don't go to the underground meeting tonight.

LASZLO

soberly
I must.
adds, with a smile
Besides, it isn't often that a man has the chance to display heroics
before his wife.

ILSA

Don't joke. After Major Strasser's warning tonight, I am frightened.

LASZLO

To tell you the truth, I am frightened, too. Shall I remain here in
our hotel room hiding, or shall I carry on the best I can?

ILSA

Whatever I'd say, you'd carry on. Victor, why don't you tell me
about Rick? What did you find out?

LASZLO

Apparently he has the letters.

ILSA

Yes?

LASZLO

But no intention of selling them. One would think if sentiment
wouldn't persuade him, money would.

ILSA

ill at ease, trying to keep her voice steady
Did he give any reason?

LASZLO

He suggested I ask you.

ILSA

Ask *me?*

LASZLO

Yes. He said, "Ask your wife." I don't know why he said that.

Ilsa walks to the bed and sits down. Laszlo turns off the light.

LASZLO

Well, our friend outside will think we've retired by now. I'll be going in a few minutes.

He sits down on the bed beside her. A silence falls between them. It grows strained. Finally,

LASZLO

quietly
Ilsa, I...

ILSA

Yes?

A pause.

LASZLO

When I was in the concentration camp, were you lonely in Paris?

Their faces are barely visible in the darkness.

ILSA

Yes, Victor, I was.

LASZLO

sympathetically
I know how it is to be lonely.
very quietly
Is there anything you wish to tell me?

ILSA

she controls herself, speaking low
No, Victor, there isn't.

There is silence.

LASZLO

I love you very much, my dear.

ILSA

barely able to speak
Yes. Yes, I know. Victor, whatever I do, will you believe that I,
that...

LASZLO

You don't even have to say it. I'll believe.

Bending down, he kisses her cheek.

LASZLO

getting up
Goodnight, dear.

ILSA

Goodnight.
watching him go
Victor!

She gets up and follows him to the door. He is just opening it. In the slit of light from the hall, we see her face, which is strained and worried. She hesitates.

ILSA

in a tone which suggests this is not what she had been tempted to say
Be careful.

LASZLO

Of course, I'll be careful.

He kisses her on the cheek and goes out the door. She stands there for a few seconds, then crosses to look out of the window. When she sees him walking down the street, she closes the blind again, gets a cloak from the bedroom and leaves.

Inside the cafe, Rick and Carl are bent over ledgers. Carl is very busy figuring.

CARL

looking up
Well, you are in pretty good shape, Herr Rick.

RICK

How long can I afford to stay closed?

CARL

Oh, two weeks, maybe three.

RICK

Maybe I won't have to. A bribe has worked before. In the meantime, everybody stays on salary.

CARL

Oh, thank you, Herr Rick. Sacha will be happy to hear it. I owe him money.

RICK

Now you finish locking up, will you, Carl?

CARL

I will. Then I am going to the meeting of the...

RICK

interrupting
Don't tell me where you're going.

CARL

with a smile
I won't.

RICK

Goodnight.

CARL

Goodnight, M'sieur Rick.

Rick walks up the stairs to his apartment. It is dark. When the door opens, light from the hall reveals a figure in the room. Rick lights a small lamp. There is Ilsa facing him, her face white but determined. Rick pauses for a moment in astonishment.

RICK

How did you get in?

ILSA

The stairs from the street.

RICK

I told you this morning you'd come around, but this is a little ahead of schedule.
with mock politeness
Well, won't you sit down?

ILSA

Richard, I had to see you.

RICK

You use "Richard" again? We're back in Paris.

ILSA

Please.

RICK

Your unexpected visit isn't connected by any chance with the letters of transit? It seems as long as I have those letters I'll never by lonely.

ILSA

looks at him directly
You can ask any price you want, but you must give me those letters.

RICK

I went all through that with your husband. It's no deal.

ILSA

I know how you feel about me, but I'm asking you to put your feelings aside for something more important.

RICK

Do I have to hear again what a great man your husband is? What an important cause he's fighting for?

ILSA

It was your cause, too. In your own way, you were fighting for the same thing.

RICK

I'm not fighting for anything anymore, except myself. I'm the only cause I'm interested in.

A pause. Ilsa deliberately takes a new approach.

ILSA

Richard, Richard, we loved each other once. If those days meant anything at all to you...

RICK

harshly
I wouldn't bring up Paris if I were you. It's poor salesmanship.

ILSA

Please. Please listen to me. If you knew what really happened, if you only knew the truth...

RICK

cuts in
I wouldn't believe you, no matter what you told me. You'd say anything now, to get what you want.

ILSA

her temper flaring, scornful
You want to feel sorry for yourself, don't you? With so much at stake, all you can think of is your own feeling. One woman has hurt you, and you take your revenge on the rest of the world. You're a, you're a coward, and a weakling.
breaks
No. Oh, Richard, I'm sorry. I'm sorry, but, but you, you are our last hope. If you don't help us, Victor Laszlo will die in Casablanca.

RICK

What of it? I'm going to die in Casablanca. It's a good spot for it.

He turns away to light a cigarette.

RICK

turning back to Ilsa
Now, if you...

He stops short as he sees Ilsa. She is holding a small revolver in her hand.

ILSA

All right. I tried to reason with you. I tried everything. Now I want those letters.

For a moment, a look of admiration comes into Rick's eyes.

ILSA

Get them for me.

RICK

I don't have to. I got them right here.

ILSA

Put them on the table.

RICK

shaking his head
No.

ILSA

For the last time, put them on the table.

RICK

If Laszlo and the cause mean so much to you, you won't stop at anything. All right, I'll make it easier for you. Go ahead and shoot. You'll be doing me a favor.

Rick walks toward Ilsa. As he reaches her, her hand drops down.

ILSA

almost hysterical
Richard, I tried to stay away. I thought I would never see you again,

that you were out of my life.

walking to the window

The day you left Paris, if you knew what I went through! If you knew how much I loved you, how much I still love you!

Rick has taken Ilsa in his arms. He presses her tight to him and kisses her passionately. She is lost in his embrace.

Sometime later, Rick watches the revolving beacon light at the airport from his window. There is a bottle of champagne on the table and two half-filled glasses. Ilsa is talking. Rick is listening intently.

RICK

And then?

ILSA

It wasn't long after we were married that Victor went back to Czechoslovakia. They needed him in Prague, but there the Gestapo were waiting for him. Just a two-line item in the paper: ''Victor Laszlo apprehended. Sent to concentration camp.'' I was frantic. For months I tried to get word. Then it came. He was dead, shot trying to escape. I was lonely. I had nothing. Not even hope. Then I met you.

RICK

Why weren't you honest with me? Why did you keep your marriage a secret?

ILSA

Oh, it wasn't my secret, Richard. Victor wanted it that way. Not even our closest friends knew about our marriage. That was his way of protecting me. I knew so much about his work, and if the Gestapo

found out I was his wife it would be dangerous for me and for those working with us.

RICK

When did you first find out he was alive?

ILSA

Just before you and I were to leave Paris together. A friend came and told me that Victor was alive. They were hiding him in a freight car on the outskirts of Paris. He was sick; he needed me. I wanted to tell you, but I, I didn't dare. I knew, I knew you wouldn't have left Paris, and the Gestapo would have caught you. So I...Well, well, you know the rest.

RICK

Huh. But it's still a story without an ending.
looks at her directly
What about now?

ILSA

Now? I don't know.
simply
I know that I'll never have the strength to leave you again.

RICK

And Laszlo?

ILSA

Oh, you'll help him now, Richard, won't you? You'll see that he gets out? Then he'll have his work, all that he's been living for.

RICK

All except one. He won't have you.

ILSA

I can't fight it anymore. I ran away from you once. I can't do it again. Oh, I don't know what's right any longer. You'll have to think for both of us, for all of us.

RICK

All right, I will. Here's looking at you, kid.

ILSA

I wish I didn't love you so much.

Laszlo and Carl are making their way through the darkness toward Rick's. The headlights of a speeding police car sweep toward them and they flatten themselves against a wall to avoid detection. The lights move past them.

CARL

I think we lost them.

LASZLO

Yes. I'm afraid they caught some of the others.

CARL

Come inside. Come.

Laszlo and Carl enter the cafe and cross toward the bar.

CARL

Come inside. I will help you. Come in here.

LASZLO

Thank you.

CARL

I will give you some water.

Inside the apartment, Rick and Ilsa hear voices below. Rick crosses to the door. Ilsa stands just in back of him. She makes a move as if to come on the balcony but Rick's arm pushes her back. She withdraws behind the door as Rick walks out to the balcony railing.

RICK

Carl, what happened?

Both Carl and Laszlo look up.

CARL

excitedly
The police break up our meeting. Herr Rick! We escaped in the last moment.

RICK

Come up here a minute.

Carl looks up wonderingly, then starts toward the stairway.

CARL

Yes, I come.

RICK

I want you to turn out the light in the rear entrance. It might attract the police.

CARL

But Sacha always puts out that light...

RICK

cutting in
Tonight he forgot.

CARL

Yes, I come, I will do it.

At the top of the stairs, Carl sees Ilsa. He asks no questions.

RICK

in a low voice
I want you to take Miss Lund home.

CARL

Yes, sir.

As Carl goes through the door, Rick starts downstairs. Laszlo is wrapping one of the small bar towels around his cut wrist. Rick looks questioningly at the injured hand.

LASZLO

It's nothing. Just a little cut. We had to get through a window.

Rick walks to the bar, picks up a bottle, and pours a drink.

RICK

Well, this might come in handy.

LASZLO

Thank you.

RICK

Had a close one, eh?

LASZLO

Yes, rather.

RICK

Don't you sometimes wonder if it's worth all this? I mean what you're fighting for?

LASZLO

We might as well question why we breathe. If we stop breathing, we'll die. If we stop fighting our enemies, the world will die.

RICK

What of it? Then it'll be out of its misery.

LASZLO

You know how you sound, M'sieur Blaine? Like a man who's trying to convince himself of something he doesn't believe in his heart. Each of us has a destiny, for good or for evil.

RICK

dryly
Yes, I get the point.

LASZLO

I wonder if you do. I wonder if you know that you're trying to escape from yourself and that you'll never succeed.

RICK

ironically
You seem to know all about my "destiny."

LASZLO

I know a good deal more about you than you suspect. I know, for instance, that you are in love with a woman.
smiles just a little
It is perhaps a strange circumstance that we both should be in love with the same woman. The first evening I came here in this cafe, I knew there was something between you and Ilsa. Since no one is to blame, I, I demand no explanation. I ask only one thing. You won't give me the letters of transit. All right. But I want my wife to be safe. I ask you as a favor to use the letters to take her away from Casablanca.

Rick looks at Laszlo incredulously.

RICK

You love her that much?

LASZLO

Apparently you think of me only as the leader of a cause. Well, I am also a human being.
looks away for a moment, then quietly
Yes, I love her that much.

At this moment there is a crashing sound at the door of the cafe, followed by the forced entry of several gendarmes. A French officer walks into the lighted area and addresses Laszlo.

FRENCH OFFICER

Mr. Laszlo?

LASZLO

Yes?

FRENCH OFFICER

You will come with us. We have a warrant for your arrest.

LASZLO

On what charge?

FRENCH OFFICER

Captain Renault will discuss that with you later.

RICK

smiles ironically
It seems that "destiny" has taken a hand.

Laszlo looks for a moment at Rick, then in dignified silence crosses to the officer. Together they walk toward the door. Rick's eyes follow them, but his expression reveals nothing of his feelings.

The next morning in Renault's office. Rick is there.

RICK

But you haven't any actual proof, and you know it. This isn't Germany or occupied France. All you can do is fine him a few thousand francs and give him thirty days. You might as well let him go now.

RENAULT

Ricky, I'd advise you not to be too interested in what happens to Laszlo. If by any chance you were to help him to escape...

RICK

cutting in
What makes you think I'd stick my neck out for Laszlo?

RENAULT

Because, one, you have bet ten thousand francs he'd escape. Two, you have the letters of transit, now don't bother to deny it. And, well, you might do it simply because you don't like Strasser's looks. As a matter of fact, I don't like him either.

RICK

Well, they're all excellent reasons.

RENAULT

Don't count too much on my friendship, Ricky. In this matter I'm powerless. Besides, I might lose the ten thousand francs.

RICK

You're not very subtle, but you are effective. I, I get the point. Yes, I have the letters, but I intend using them myself. I'm leaving Casablanca on tonight's plane, the last plane.

RENAULT

Huh?

RICK

And I'm taking a friend with me.

smiles
One you'll appreciate.

RENAULT

What friend?

RICK

Ilsa Lund.

An amazed incredulity is written on Renault's face.

RICK

That ought to put your mind to rest about my helping Laszlo escape.
The last man I want to see in America.

RENAULT

shrewdly
You didn't come here to tell me this. You have the letters of transit.
You can fill in your name and hers and leave any time you please.
Why are you still interested in what happens to Laszlo?

RICK

I'm not. But I *am* interested in what happens to Ilsa and me. We
have a legal right to go, that's true. But people have been held in
Casablanca in spite of their legal rights.

RENAULT

What makes you think we want to hold you?

RICK

Ilsa is Laszlo's wife. She probably knows things that Strasser would
like to know. Louis, I'll make a deal with you. Instead of this petty

charge you have against him, you can get something really big, something that would chuck him in a concentration camp for years. That would be quite a feather in your cap, wouldn't it?

RENAULT

It certainly would. Germany…
corrects himself
Vichy would be very grateful.

RICK

Then release him. You be at my place a half an hour before the plane leaves. I'll arrange to have Laszlo come there to pick up the letters of transit, and that'll give you the criminal grounds on which to make the arrest. You get him, and we get away. To the Germans that last will be just a minor annoyance.

RENAULT

puzzled
There's still something about this business I don't quite understand. Miss Lund, she's very beautiful, yes, but you were never interested in any woman.

RICK

Well, she isn't just any woman.

RENAULT

I see. How do I know you'll keep your end of the bargain?

RICK

I'll make the arrangements right now with Laszlo in the visitor's pen.

RENAULT

Ricky, I'm going to miss you. Apparently you're the only one in Casablanca who has even less scruples than I.

RICK

dryly
Oh, thanks.

RENAULT

Go ahead, Ricky.

RICK

And by the way, call off your watchdogs when you let him go. I don't want them around this afternoon. I'm taking no chances, Louis, not even with you.

A waiter at the Blue Parrot is bringing coffee into Ferrari's office. Rick and Ferrari are sitting there.

FERRARI

Shall we draw up papers, or is our handshake good enough?

RICK

It's certainly not good enough. But since I'm in a hurry, it'll have to do.

FERRARI

Oh, to get out of Casablanca and go to America! You're a lucky man.

RICK

Oh, by the way, my agreement with Sam's always been that he gets twenty-five percent of the profits. That still goes.

FERRARI

Hm. I happen to know he gets ten percent. But he's worth twenty-five.

RICK

And Abdul and Carl and Sacha, they stay with the place, or I don't sell.

FERRARI

Of course they stay. Rick's wouldn't be Rick's without them.

RICK

getting up
Well, so long.
he walks to the door, stops, turns
Don't forget, you owe Rick's a hundred cartons of American cigarettes.

FERRARI

I shall remember to pay it to myself.

Rick leaves. Ferrari swats a fly on the table.

Outside Rick's Cafe, a huge placard is pasted on the door:

CLOSED
By Order of the Prefect of Police

Someone knocks on the door. Rick is seated at a table inside reading the letters of transit. When he hears the knock, he puts them away in his pocket and goes to the door. It is Renault.

RICK

You're late.

RENAULT

I was informed just as Laszlo was about to leave the hotel, so I knew I would be on time.

RICK

I thought I asked you to tie up your watch-dogs.

RENAULT

Oh, he won't be followed here.
looks around the empty cafe
You know, this place will never be the same without you, Ricky.

RICK

Yes, I know what you mean, but I've already spoken to Ferrari. You'll still win at roulette.

RENAULT

Is everything ready?

RICK

tapping his breast pocket
I have the letters right here.

RENAULT

Tell me, when we searched the place, where were they?

RICK

Sam's piano.

RENAULT

Serves me right for not being musical!
The sound of a car pulling up is heard.

RICK

Oh. Here they are. You'd better wait in my office.
Renault walks up to the office. Outside, Laszlo is paying the cab-driver. Ilsa is walking toward the entrance.

LASZLO

to the cabdriver
Here.

Inside, Rick opens the door. Ilsa rushes in. Her intensity reveals the strain she is under.

ILSA

Richard, Victor thinks I'm leaving with him. Haven't you told him?

RICK

No, not yet.

ILSA

But it's all right, isn't it? You were able to arrange everything?

RICK

Everything is quite all right.

ILSA

Oh, Rick!
She looks at him with a vaguely questioning look.

RICK

We'll tell him at the airport. The less time to think, the easier for all of us. Please trust me.

ILSA

Yes, I will.

Laszlo comes in.

LASZLO

M'sieur Blaine. I don't know how to thank you.

RICK

Oh, save it. We've still lots of thinks to do.

LASZLO

I brought the money, M'sieur Blaine.

RICK

Keep it. You'll need it in America.

LASZLO

But we made a deal.

RICK

cutting him short
Oh, never mind about that. You won't have any trouble in Lisbon, will you?

LASZLO

No. It's all arranged.

RICK

Good. I've got the letters right here, all made out in blank.
takes out the letters
All you have to do is fill in the signatures.

He hands them to Laszlo, who takes them gratefully.

RENAULT'S VOICE

Victor Laszlo!
Renault is at the bottom of the stairs.

RENAULT

Victor Laszlo, you are under arrest on a charge of accessory to the murder of the couriers from whom these letters were stolen.
Ilsa and Laszlo are both caught completely off guard. They turn toward Rick. Horror is in Ilsa's eyes. Renault takes the letters.

RENAULT

Oh, you are surprised about my friend, Ricky? The explanation is quite simple. Love, it seems, has triumphed over virtue. Thank...

Obviously, the situation delights Renault. He is smiling as he turns toward Rick. Suddenly the smile fades. In Rick's hand is a gun which he is leveling at Renault.

RICK

Not so fast, Louis. Nobody's going to be arrested. Not for a while yet.

RENAULT

Have you taken leave of your senses?

RICK

I have. Sit down over there.

Renault hesitates, then walks toward Rick.

RENAULT

Put that gun down.

RICK

putting his hand up to stop Renault
Louis, I wouldn't like to shoot you, but I will, if you take one more
step.

Renault halts for a moment and studies Rick.

RENAULT

Under the circumstances, I will sit down.

He walks to a table and sits down.

RICK

sharply
Keep your hands on the table.

RENAULT

I suppose you know what you're doing, but I wonder if you realize
what this means?

RICK

I do. We've got plenty of time to discuss that later.

RENAULT

reproachfully, to Rick
"Call off your watch-dogs," you said.

RICK

Just the same, you call the airport and let me hear you tell them.
And remember, this gun's pointed right at your heart.

RENAULT

as he dials
That is my least vulnerable spot.

Rick takes back the letters.

RENAULT

into the phone
Hello, is that the airport? This is Captain Renault speaking. There'll
be two letters of transit for the Lisbon plane. There's to be no trouble about them. Good.

*In the German consulate, Strasser is jiggling the telephone receiver
violently.*

STRASSER

Hello? Hello?
*He hangs up the receiver momentarily, presses a buzzer on his desk,
then again lifts the receiver.*

STRASSER

to an officer entering
My car, quickly!

OFFICER

Zu Befehl, Herr Major.

The officer exits and Strasser resumes on the telephone.

STRASSER

This is Major Strasser. Have a squad of police meet me at the airport at once. At once! Do you hear?

Hanging up the receiver, and grabbing his cap, he hurriedly exits.

*At the airport, the outline of the transport plane is barely visible.
A uniformed orderly is at the telephone near the hangar door.*

ORDERLY

Hello. Hello, radio tower? Lisbon plane taking off in ten minutes.
East runway. Visibility: one and a half miles. Light ground fog.
Depth of fog: approximately 500. Ceiling: unlimited. Thank you.

*He hangs up, and crosses to the car that has just pulled up. Renault
gets out, closely followed by Rick, hand in pocket, still covering
Renault with a gun. Laszlo and Ilsa come from the rear of the car.*

RICK

indicating the orderly
Louis, have your man go with Mr. Laszlo and take care of his
luggage.

RENAULT

bows ironically
Certainly Rick. Anything you say.
to orderly
Find Mr. Laszlo's luggage and put it on the plane.

ORDERLY

Yes, sir. This way please.

The orderly escorts Laszlo off in the direction of the plane. Rick takes the letters of transit out of his pocket, and hands them to Renault.

RICK

If you don't mind, you fill in the names
smiles
That will make it even more official.

RENAULT

You think of everything, don't you?

RICK

quietly
And the names are Mr. and Mrs. Victor Laszlo.

Both Ilsa and Renault look at Rick with astonishment.

ILSA

But why *my* name, Richard?

RICK

watching Renault
Because you're getting on that plane.

ILSA

dazed
I don't understand. What about you?

RICK

I'm staying here with him 'til the plane gets safely away.

ILSA

as Rick's intention fully dawns on her

No, Richard, no. What has happened to you? Last night we said...

RICK

Last night we said a great many things. You said I was to do the thinking for both of us. Well, I've done a lot of it since then and it all adds up to one thing. You're getting on that plane with Victor where you belong.

ILSA

protesting
But Richard, no, I, I...

RICK

Now you've got to listen to me. Do you have any idea what you'd have to look forward to if you stayed here? Nine chances out of ten we'd both wind up in a concentration camp. Isn't that true, Louis?

RENAULT

as he countersigns the papers
I am afraid that Major Strasser would insist.

ILSA

turns to Rick
You're saying this only to make me go.

RICK

I'm saying it because it's true. Inside of us we both know you belong with Victor. You're part of his work, the thing that keeps him going. If that plane leaves the ground and you're not with him, you'll regret it.

ILSA

No.

RICK

Maybe not today, maybe not tomorrow, but soon, and for the rest of your life.

ILSA

But what about us?

RICK

We'll always have Paris. We didn't have it, we'd lost it, until you came to Casablanca. We got it back last night.

ILSA

And I said I would never leave you!

RICK

And you never will. But I've got a job to do, too. Where I'm going you can't follow. What I've got to do, you can't be any part of. Ilsa, I'm no good at being noble, but it doesn't take much to see that the problems of three little people don't amount to a hill of beans in this crazy world. Someday you'll understand that. Not now. Here's looking at you, kid.

At this moment, Laszlo comes back.

LASZLO

Everything is in order?

RICK

All except one thing. There's something you should know before you leave.

LASZLO

sensing what is coming
Monsieur Blaine, I don't ask you to explain anything.

RICK

I'm going to anyway, because it may make a difference to you later on. You said you knew about Ilsa and me.

LASZLO

Yes.

RICK

But you didn't know she was at my place last night when you were. She came there for the letters of transit. Isn't that true, Ilsa?

ILSA

facing Laszlo
Yes.

RICK

his voice more harsh, almost brutal
She tried everything to get them, and nothing worked. She did her best to convince me that she was still in love with me, but that was all over long ago. For your sake, she pretended it wasn't, and I let her pretend.

LASZLO

I understand.
Rick hands him the letters.

RICK

Here it is.

LASZLO

Thanks. I appreciate it. And welcome back to the fight. This time
I know our side will win.
On the field, the airplane propellers start turning.

LASZLO

Are you ready, Ilsa?

Ilsa looks at Rick for the last time.

ILSA

Yes, I'm ready.
to Rick
Goodbye, Rick. God bless you.

RICK

You better hurry, or you'll miss that plane.

*As Ilsa and Laszlo leave in the direction of the plane, Renault regards
Rick triumphantly.*

RENAULT

Well, I was right! You *are* a sentimentalist!

RICK

Stay where you are! I don't know what you're talking about.

RENAULT

What you just did for Laszlo, and that fairy tale you invented to send Ilsa away with him. I know a little about women, my friend. She went, but she knew you were lying.

RICK

Anyway, thanks for helping me out.

Rick's face reveals nothing.

RENAULT

I suppose you know this isn't going to be very pleasant for either of us, especially for you. I'll have to arrest you, of course.

RICK

As soon as the plane goes, Louis.

As the door to the plane is finally closed, Strasser's car screeches to a halt in front of the hangar. Strasser jumps out of the car and runs toward Renault.

STRASSER

What was the meaning of that phone call?

RENAULT

Victor Laszlo is on that plane.

He nods off down the field. Strasser turns to see the plane taxiing toward the runway.

STRASSER

Why do you stand here? Why don't you stop him?

RENAULT

Ask M'sieur Rick.

Strasser looks briefly at Rick, then makes a step toward the telephone just inside the hangar door. Rick points the revolver at Strasser.

RICK

Get away from that phone!

Strasser stops in his tracks, looks at Rick, and sees that he means business.

STRASSER

steely
I would advise you not to interfere.

RICK

I was willing to shoot Captain Renault, and I'm willing to shoot you.

Strasser runs toward the telephone. He desperately grabs the receiver.

STRASSER

into phone
Hello?

RICK

Put that phone down!

STRASSER

Get me the Radio Tower!

RICK

Put it down!

Strasser, his one hand holding the receiver, pulls out a pistol with the other hand and shoots quickly at Rick. The bullet misses, but Rick's shot has hit Strasser, who crumples to the ground.

A police car speeds up to the hangar. Four gendarmes jump out. In the distance, the plane is turning onto the runway. The gendarmes run to Renault. Renault turns to them.

GENDARME

Mon Capitaine!

RENAULT

Major Strasser's been shot.
pauses as he looks at Rick, then to the gendarmes
Round up the usual suspects.

GENDARME

Oui, mon Capitaine.

He leads the other gendarmes off. The two men look at one another. Renault picks up a bottle of Vichy water and opens it.

RENAULT

Well, Rick, you're not only a sentimentalist, but you've become a patriot.

RICK

Maybe, but it seemed like a good time to start.

RENAULT

I think perhaps you're right.

As he pours the water into a glass, Renault sees the Vichy label and quickly drops the bottle into a trash basket which he then kicks over.

Rick and Renault watch the plane take off, maintaining their gaze until it disappears into the clouds.

RENAULT

It might be a good idea for you to disappear from Casablanca for a while. There's a Free French garrison over at Brazzaville. I could be induced to arrange a passage.

RICK

smiles
My letter of transit? I could use a trip. But it doesn't make any difference about our bet. You still owe me ten thousand francs.

RENAULT

And that ten thousand francs should pay our expenses.

RICK

Our expenses!

RENAULT

Uh huh.

RICK

Louis, I think this is the beginning of a beautiful friendship.

Rick and Renault walk off together into the night.

THE END

COMMENTARY
AND ANALYSIS

CHARLES CHAMPLIN
RICHARD CORLISS
ROGER EBERT
UMBERTO ECO
ALJEAN HARMETZ
J. HOBERMAN

CHARLES CHAMPLIN

THOUGHTS ON CASABLANCA

IN THE DAYS of my youth I merely thought *Casablanca* was a wonderful movie—exciting, hopelessly romantic and very satisfying. Humphrey Bogart was the man who more than any other I wanted to be and who, in occasional fantasies, I imagined I was. Ingrid Bergman was the woman I wanted to love and protect from all dangers. At first, Paul Henreid did not really fit into my calculations. The idea of the noble sacrifice was quite new to me then, but I caught on quickly and, having toyed with the idea that Henreid instead of Bogart should have gone off to Brazzaville with Claude Rains, I realized that things had to work out as they did, and I felt better for accepting the fact.

A half-century later, I love *Casablanca* not a whit less, probably even more because, like all the movies we loved in our youth, it now carries a rich frosting of personal associations and a sweet melancholy, born of the intimations of mortality—the viewer's own, confirmed as it were by the passage of the film's wondrous stars.

And, after a half-century, I can see *Casablanca,* at least a little more objectively, as the apotheosis of the Hollywood romantic melodrama, a kind of fearless and perfected make-believe that you probably couldn't get away with today. Singing the *Marseillaise* in the face of the snarling Gestapo men! As I am frequently told (as if it were somehow my fault), they don't make movies like that any more. It's true, they don't, and I explain sadly that it's because they don't make the world the way they used to, either. Romantic idealism doesn't come as easily as once it did. Information, and rather too much of it, has led us toward being, in Oscar Wilde's formulation, cynics who know the price of everything and the value of nothing. We can't play make-believe the way we used to, and the loss is ours. Out of wartime reality, Howard Koch and the Epstein brothers, Philip and Julius, constructed a beautiful, tragic, heroic dream and no small part of its appeal now is that it arose and reflected a world in which things seemed to be simpler and clearer. (Whether they were or not is irrelevant.)

Thirty viewings later (at least), I still can't watch only a little of *Casablanca;* I have to stay aboard until Brazzaville. And I can't watch any of it without a tightening of the throat and a hint of moisture in the eyes, sighing for the kind of immortality the movies provide their stars and the savor they lend to our more transient lives.

CHARLES CHAMPLIN hosts ''Champlin on Film'' on Bravo Cable. He recently retired as arts editor and columnist of *The Los Angeles Times,* where he was also principal film critic 1967–80.

CASABLANCA:
AN ANALYSIS OF THE FILM

WHEN *CASABLANCA* FIRST APPEARED, toward the end of 1942, few movie-wise people would have bet that screen history was about to be embossed on the Warner Brothers shield. Hal Wallis had a topical subject on which to base another hit production—but everybody was making war-effort movies. Moreover, the final script—which bore some unrecognizable traces of *Everybody Comes to Rick's,* "one of the world's worst plays" according to James Agee—had been written at breakneck speed and under appalling pressure by a junior member of the Warners writing pool, Howard Koch, after the studio's prolific Epstein brothers had made their contributions and had moved on to another, presumably more important assignment.

Although *Casablanca* defines Bogie for all time as the existential-hero-in-spite-of-himself, several of his roles just preceding this one (notably *High Sierra* and *The Maltese Falcon*) had prepared his fans for the misanthropy and climactic selflessness he would embody as Rick Blaine. Bergman (as Ilsa Lund) and Henreid (as Victor Laszlo) are hardly incandescent lovers—neither are Bergman and Bogart, for that matter—but their very turgidity as sexual partners works, intentionally or not, to the film's advantage. Claude Rains had played a perplexing variety of roles: some sympathetic (*Now, Voyager*), some unsympathetic (*Crime Without Passion*), and some in which he was a good man weak enough to fall prey to overwhelming forces (scientific megalomania in *The Invisible Man,* political corruption in *Mr. Smith Goes to Washington*); audiences weren't sure of the proper moral attitude to assume toward Rains, and this made him perfect for the suave, enigmatic Louis Renault. The outrageously dense supporting cast of Conrad Veidt, Peter Lorre, Sidney Greenstreet, Dooley Wilson, S. Z. Sakall, Leonid Kinskey, John Qualen, Curt Bois, Marcel Dalio, and dozens of others would have lent a certain spurious sense of resonance to *A History of the Blue Movie,* let alone to a film in which each player is adroitly cast and allowed a privileged moment or two all his own. Michael Curtiz had directed forty-two films in the previous decade for Warners and, when one considers the restrictions on shot-planning and script-doctoring inherent in such a prodigious output, the generally high quality of his work is impressive. Undoubtedly, much of the film's verve and terse efficiency—as well as its occasionally hurried, perfunctory *mise-en-scène*—can be traced to Curtiz.

But the success of *Casablanca* ultimately derives from the character development and dialogue. Warners would again assemble attractive casts, and assign Curtiz to direct them—as with *Passage to Marseilles.* None of the sequels was as richly textured, as effortlessly witty, as complex in characterization, as entertaining or, consequently, as popular as *Casablanca.* On the other hand, when Koch had the opportunity, five years later, to work with Max Ophuls on *Letter from an Unknown Woman,* he produced a script as drenched in delicate Viennese irony as *Casablanca* was suffused with the more pungent irony of an occupied city where all roles are uncertain, and thus played to the hilt—and where the only values are the shifting ones of the Vichy franc, and thus gambled on with a desperation that tries to pass for insouciance.

I

The vigorous stoicism with which Rick Blaine surrenders Ilsa to Laszlo, and the pleasure he exudes in walking with Renault into the final fade-out, have given rise to two seductive theories about the film, one pertinent and one impertinent. The first is that *Casablanca* is a political allegory, with Rick as President Roosevelt (*casa blanca* is Spanish for "white house"), a man who gambles on the odds of going to war until circumstance and his own submerged nobility force him to close his casino (read: partisan politics) and commit himself— first by financing the Side of Right and then by fighting for it. The time of the film's action (December, 1941) adds credence to this view, as does the irrelevant fact that, two months after *Casablanca* opened, Roosevelt (Rick) and Prime Minister Winston Churchill (Laszlo) met for a war conference in Casablanca.

The other theory proposes *Casablanca* as a repressed homosexual fantasy, in which Rick rejects his token mistress for an honest if furtive affair with another man. Now, Rick is hardly "rough trade," and Renault's exhaustive string of conquests attests to his performance, if not his preference. Still, they make an intriguing active-passive pair. Renault flirts with Rick—indeed, he flirts with everyone—throughout the film, and at one point he tells Ilsa, "He is the kind of man that ...well, if I were a woman, and *I* were not around, I should be in love with Rick." The pansexual sophistica- tion that began in the Seventies makes such inferences as these appealing, especially when we can attach them to artifacts from our own primitive past. But we should be careful when we paint yester- day's picture in today's colors; tomorrow they may seem gaudily inappropriate. At the time Renault speaks to Ilsa, he doesn't know that she was and is "in love with Rick." Ilsa, however, loves an idealized Rick—a socialist adventurer, who fought on the right sides in Ethiopia and Spain—while Renault loves or likes or admires the real Rick, who uses his financial and sexual authority to throw Nazis out of his café and idealists out of his life (the latter more gently, to be sure). For Rick, women are an occasional obsession; for Renault they are a perpetual diversion. Both want companionship more than they need love. If audiences did not intuit this preference, they wouldn't accept the film's ending with such supreme satisfaction.

Besides, Renault's presumed ambisexuality is of less interest than his genuine ambiguity. When Renault's tongue is not in his cheek (a place of relative repose), it is darting out to catch the weary or unwary females who buzz into Casablanca hoping for a visa. Renault is not rapacious so much as he is pleased by the power that he wields and amused at the indignities men must endure—and women must enjoy—for him to use that power to their benefit. He is radiantly corrupt. He has style. What Rick thinks of, early in the film, as political realism, Renault knows is expediency. In Rick, American pragmatism has soured into phlegmatism, while in Renault, French charm has degenerated into coquetry. But Rick can give Renault a sense of values, and Renault can give Rick a sense of proportion; both have a sardonic sense of humor. In Jungian terms, Rick is the *animus* of this split personality and Renault is the *anima*. Or, as they used to say at Schwabb's, the two are made for each other.

Rick and Renault share the economic and spiritual leadership of Vichy-ruled Casablanca with Signor Ferrari (Sidney Greenstreet), the black-market boss who can say simply, "As leader of all illegal activities in Casablanca, I am an influential and respected man." This odd troika presides over a populace that is either flourishing or desperate, depending on their ability to hustle persuasively, and regardless of their former status. Thus, a beautiful woman tells her companion, an old letch: "It used to take a villa at Cannes, or the very least, a string of pearls. Now all I ask is an exit visa." (Her plight was even more serious than she had feared: her dialogue was cut from the completed film.) When the manager of "the second largest banking house in Amsterdam" tries to bribe Carl, the head-waiter, for a drink with Rick, Carl replies that "the leading banker is the pastry chef in our kitchen," and pockets the money. Carl, whom the script describes as the author of books on "mathematics... astronomy...the greatest professor in the whole University of Leipzig," represents the humanistic—that is, the Jewish—side of the German psyche.

Of Rick's other employees, the bartender (Leonid Kinskey) had been "the Czar's favorite sword-swallower"; Abdul the doorman

(Dan Seymour) adds some local color to the café, if not to the film; and the croupier of Rick's iliegal gambling table is given no specific past, but since he is played by Marcel Dalio, reverberations of his tainted aristocracy in *The Rules of the Game* may appear on the seismographic memories of some moviegoers. The only member of Rick's retinue who indicates any integrity with his own past is Sam, the piano player (Dooley Wilson), who had been Rick's companion four years earlier in Paris—when Rick and Ilsa fell in love—and shares the same relationship with him in Casablanca. The continuity of Sam's function suggests that the light-hearted Rick of Paris and the pessimistic Rick of Casablanca are closer to one another than his crude bitterness toward Ilsa later on in the café would imply. At any rate, Rick's role to the rest of his staff is that of the curt if protective patriarch, whereas he shows Sam a courtesy that he reveals to few others, usually prefacing requests with a gentlemanly ''do you mind.'' Indeed, Ferrari's offer to ''buy'' Sam, along with Rick's saloon, drives Rick to a rare flight of self-righteousness—''I don't buy or sell human beings''—which leads us to believe that, at this point in the film at least, Sam is one of the few beings in Casablanca whom Rick would consider human.

II

After a brief montage of animated maps describing the European émigré's route through Casablanca, the film's irony and the city's duplicity are immediately established with the entrance of the Dark European (Curt Bois). The term is both literal and metaphorical: this guy is doubly shady, pursuing the pickpocket's profession by warning his suckers, with a great show of concern, about the many pickpockets in town. With a pithiness typical of both the characters and the dialogue, the writers not only establish the sinister dexterity of this Dark European—an, by extension, of all those who flourish in Casablanca—but also impart some crucial plot information. ''Two German couriers were found murdered in the desert. (*With an ironic smile* [says the script]) The...unoccupied desert.'' They had been carrying letters of transit—visas which cannot be questioned—papers whose fateful power will bring all who touch them close to death, like the sexual love that turns to syphilis in Schnitzler's *La Ronde*.

The sign by the door of Captain Renault's *Palais de Justice*—itself an ironic title—reads *"Liberté, Egalité, Fraternité."* The film will place a fairly grave accent on Liberty (as personified by Ilsa and Laszlo) and a cute accent on Fraternity (as exemplified by Rick and Renault). As for equality...well, this is an African country run by white Europeans; there is a Dark European in the film, but no blackamoor. Economic and sexual equality are also ignored. In the words of the Dark European, ''The rich and beautiful sail to Lisbon. The poor are always with us.''

Even Major Strasser (Conrad Veidt), Laszlo's formidable pursuer and the chief representative of the Third Reich's arrogance and humorlessness, is entertaining in a verminous way—a quality that would be lacking later Hollywood Nazis, once the makers of war movies decided that putting a two- or three-dimensional villain on the screen was a creative act of treason. Strasser can't help but be affected by the irony that laces Casablanca's humid air, and he occasionally jousts with Renault and, later, with Rick and Laszlo. But he always loses in these contests of wit, if only because of his grim, heavy-handed determination to win.

Whenever a long-lost love emerges from the machine-made mists of a Hollywood hero's past, an ''other woman'' is needed to add a little dramatic tension to the confrontation in the present. Rick's present is clouded by such a smoke-screen of cynicism that an alluring third party would be redundant—but one is provided anyway: Yvonne. Her main function, aside from ever-so-tenuously indicating Rick's vacillation between German power and Allied positive thinking, is to act as foil for two of *Casablanca*'s most quoted lines. More than any other, this bit of dialogue established Rick and Bogart as early existential heroes.

YVONNE: Where were you last night?
RICK: That's so long ago, I don't remember.
YVONNE (after a pause): Will I see you tonight?
RICK: I never make plans that far ahead.

With the merest suggestion that his stoic rejection of Yvonne will save her a lot of heartache (and save him a few annoying hysteria scenes), Rick sends her home—with Sacha, who really loves her. Rick seems to throw away women with the same assured carelessness he evinces in throwing away lines; but there is hardly ever a wasted motion in either his actions or his dialogue. Here he has obliquely stated his philosophy, ended a tedious affair, and made a match. He has also lured Renault into the conversation, for the Captain, after chiding Rick on his extravagance with women (Rains says, "Someday they may be scarce," but the original line is wittier and more relevant: "Someday they may be rationed"), allows that he is interested in Yvonne himself. Rick, it would seem, can have any woman he wants—and yet he doesn't seem to want any.

RENAULT: I have often speculated on why you don't return to America. Did you abscond with the church funds? Did you run off with a Senator's wife? I like to think you killed a man. It is the romantic in me.
RICK (sardonically): It was a combination of all three.

For some, Casablanca is a purgatory where their worldly sins— money, jewels, political connections—must be bartered away in order to get out. For others—the omnipresent but unseen poor—Casablanca is sheer hell, with no hope of redemption. For Rick it is Limbo, a state of suspended spiritual animation. We never do find out about Rick's distant past, although he finds out about Ilsa's; perhaps this is one reason why the Bogart character lives today, while Bergman's Ilsa has lost co-starred billing in the minds of *Casablanca*'s devotees to Rick's partner in enigmatic ambiguity, Louis Renault. But while Rick's sardonic evasion doesn't tell us about his past, it does portend future events which only he can control. The film's climax will have Rick "abscond with the church funds" by selling his saloon to Ferrari, "run off with a Senator's wife" by leaving Casablanca in the company of the coquettish representative from Vichy, and "kill a man"—Major Strasser.

> RENAULT: And what in heaven's name brought you to Casablanca?
> RICK: My health. I came to Casablanca for the waters.
> RENAULT: Waters? What waters? We're in the desert.
> RICK: I was misinformed.

The Pinteresque understatement of Rick's ludicrous "explanation" telegraphs to Renault elements of pastness that point to his reluctance to explain himself. And yet there is some truth in his nimble evasion, as we will discover. Some years before, Rick was "misinformed." *That* sent him away from Paris, and eventually brought him to Casablanca.

Rick is even nimbler, and more oblique, about his dormant political nobility. We know he ran guns to Ethiopia in 1935, and fought for the Loyalists in 1936, long-shot activities that make his current political and sexual neutrality look more counter-revolutionary than it would otherwise. But when Strasser tries to intimidate Rick by reading him a Nazi-researched dossier of these adventures, Rick simply glances at the German's little black book and, with a bland expression that perfectly reveals his contempt for the obviousness of Strasser's methods, asks, "Are my eyes really brown?" This blending of the modest and the arrogant, the casual and the ballsy, stamps Rick as a man of courage as indelibly as will his climactic heroism. For here he has nothing to gain by his bravado except an affirmation of his self-respect—and an off-hand solicitation of Renault's respect, which one doubts Rick values very highly. Nevertheless, when Renault (in the same conversation) says of Laszlo, "Of course, one must admit he has great courage," it is a tribute that Rick has already earned for himself.

Laszlo *is* courageous. True, the oratorical skills necessary in a Resistance leader—not to mention his lame-duck role in the plot—frequently draw him into pomposity and self-righteousness. But Laszlo can be ironic when irony is needed, if only to Advance The Cause. (Humorless men, like Laszlo, like Strasser, indeed like Charles Foster Kane, can use humor to their advantage: to convert, to threaten, to *seem* human. These three men, superficially so different, are tied together by their use of power and people. They are all public men; only their goals distinguish them.) Thus, when an underground contact (John Qualen) tells Laszlo that he has "read five times that you were killed in five different places," Laszlo replies, *(smiling wryly)* "As you can see, it was true every single time." In fact, the life of a fugitive has sapped enough of Laszlo's strength so that he must channel all of it into politics, and too little of it to his love, his wife, Ilsa.

Four years earlier, in pre-Occupation Paris, Ilsa had been only a mystery woman ("I know so little about you—just the fact that you had your teeth straightened"). Now, in Casablanca, she is a phantom. Once she had been the repository of Rick's romantic love and political idealism, to such an extent that distinctions between personal obsessions and political affections blurred and then merged. When the Nazis moved into Paris, she moved out of his life; Rick's idealism and love, because they had become inseparable, were fatally dissolved on the same day. The death of romance left a rancid crust of cynicism upon Rick's soul, and over the years the crust hardened to form a casket for his optimism and nobility. The crucial dramatic question is whether her reappearance after such a long time—a lifetime, a death time—will help revive that Parisian optimism or bury it for good; and whether, once Ilsa has resurrected Rick's romantic love and political idealism, he will be able to suppress the former for the sake of the latter.

In the 1937 flashback, Rick bombards Ilsa with the kind of questions his Casablanca acquaintances would later ask him: "Who are you really, and what were you before? What did you do, and what did you think?" His famous toast—"Here's looking at you, kid"—

can be read as meaning, "Here's trying to look into your soul, kid, to figure out who you really are." For most of *Casablanca,* Rick and Ilsa and Laszlo are defined not only by their pasts but by the suspicions other characters have about these pasts. Ilsa in 1937 and Rick in 1941 are evasive for the same reason: for each, a love affair melded into international affairs so imperceptibly and so relentlessly that telling one's confession would sound like a chaotic, personalized history lesson. The film's *denouement* will, for Rick, be literally that—an "unraveling" of future conditional from past imperfect, of Western Civilization from autobiography, of duty from love.

Ilsa is basically a simple country girl; *her* irony is platitudinous. "With the whole world crumbling, we pick this time to fall in love," she says to Rick in Paris (it will be as appropriate in Casablanca). And "Was that cannon fire, or was it the pounding of my heart?" Ilsa is the sort of serious, naive young woman who would express the most exalted of emotions in the rhetoric of a Hollywood love story—unlike Rick and Renault, whose diction and delivery indicate a more genuine, more assured compatibility.

As signposts to the film's plot and characterization, these lines have meanings they lack as stabs at rapier wit. When Ilsa dodges Rick's probes into her past and his demands on her future (even saying, in response to Rick's suggestion that they get married as soon as they arrive in Marseilles, that "That's too far ahead to plan"), she is unknowingly clarifying Rick's abrupt dismissal of Yvonne: Rick's quest for a past and hope for a future with Ilsa had inflamed a love that disappointment turned to ashes—"once burned, twice shy." When she tells Rick that "you must leave Paris" and he replies, "No, *we* must leave," Ilsa is preparing the viewer for Rick's final choice of the greatest good for the greatest number over an easy solution to "the problems of three little people."

Of course, Rick leaves Paris alone, with the Paris rain smudging Ilsa's farewell letter as a considerate substitute for Rick's (and Bogart's) reluctant tears. The flashback ends with drunkenly bleary instead of heroically teary—the cynic's attempt to becloud pain with a dull gauze rather than letting it all drip out. When Ilsa interrupts Rick's masochistic reverie to tell him about her marriage to Laszlo then and now, Rick accuses her of literal and political prostitution—the loser's attempt to punish himself by hurting someone he may still love. As Ilsa walks out, Rick surrenders to one of those rare waste motions that reveal the unwinding of his coiled composure: he collapses, heart-broken and instantly hung-over, like the sort of drunk ''M'sieur Rick'' would throw out of his café without breaking his stride, his composure, or the silky pattern of his dialogue.

III

The galaxy of supporting characters in *Casablanca* constitute a dazzling, baroque hall of mirrors that reflect facets and distortions of the leading characters' lives and life-styles. Ugarte and Ferrari are various corruptions of Rick, as peddler and panderer, respectively; Carl is a cuddly, less ostentatious Laszlo; Sacha is an unseductive Renault; Yvonne and the Dark European share Rick's indecision between Free France and the Third Reich; Strasser is a German version of Renault, a prosaic scientist of war to Renault's master of the boudoir arts, the crazy-mirror image of an *übermensch* as opposed to Renault's *homme moyen sensuel.* The film is almost symphonic in the way its reflections of plot and reverberations of dialogue help to reinforce themes and deepen our understanding of Rick and Renault, Ilsa and Laszlo. One of these variations which almost amounts to a subplot, involves Rick and Annina, a young Bulgarian woman determined to get herself and her calf-like husband to America—even if it means meeting Captain Renault's stiff price. Annina's plea to Rick for advice is practically a *précis* of the film's dilemma.

> ANNINA: M'sieur, you are a man. If someone loved you very much, so that your happiness was the only thing that she wanted in the whole world but she did a bad thing to make certain of it, could you forgive her?

RICK: Nobody ever loved me that much.

ANNINA: And he never knew and the girl kept this bad thing locked in her heart? That would be all right, wouldn't it?

RICK *(harshly)*: You want my advice?

ANNINA: Oh, yes, please.

RICK: Go back to Bulgaria.

There's nothing neat about the analogy of subplot to plot here. What is clear is that the Rick-Annina dialogue acts both as echo and as presentiment. Annina's forthrightness and bravery, as much as anything else, convince Rick that he should revise his estimation of Ilsa's attachment for him; perhaps, at the moment he mutters "nobody ever loved me that much," Rick realizes how much Ilsa loved and admired him—enough to believe he had the strength to survive a bitterly cruel disillusionment. Rick "never knew"; Ilsa "kept this bad thing locked in her heart"; and ultimately she "went back" to Czechoslovakia in the person of Victor Laszlo. Of course, Ilsa didn't guarantee Rick's (or Laszlo's) happiness by leaving him to join Laszlo. And, when she comes to his apartment later to get the letters of transit, it won't be because she loves Laszlo "very much," at least not romantically, or even personally: only as the embodiment of a great cause. Indeed, as she finally realizes, she loves Rick beyond all scruple—unaware that Rick will settle for her admiration. The Rick-Annina analogy is more fitting as a portent of this climactic decision of Rick's, to send Ilsa away with Laszlo, for Rick, by fixing the roulette wheel, helps Annina get the visa money without capitulating to the *capitaine*.

Renault has his revenge when, at the suggestion of Major Strasser, he orders Rick's saloon closed. Earlier, Renault had told Rick that he allowed the place to stay open partly because Rick let him win at roulette. By assisting Annina, Rick made Renault lose. Now, Renault gestures dramatically toward the back room he has patronized for so long and says, "I'm shocked—*shocked* to find that there is gambling going on in here!" Thus, in one foul sweep, Renault satisfies Strasser with a genuine excuse for closing Rick's indicates to Rick, through the absurdity of the charge, that it was Strasser's idea to close it, and not his; and pleases himself by taking revenge on Rick for depriving him of an evening's horizontal pleasure.

The café shut down, Ilsa returns for the letters of transit which she knows are in Rick's possession. Every ploy she tries—invoking the name of the Resistance, stirring the ashes of their Paris affair, calling him a coward, pleading with him, and finally threatening him—aggravates her barely suppressed hysterical love and increases his morose fatalism. "Go ahead and shoot," Rick says. "You'll be doing me a favor." It is here that Ilsa realizes, now how much she overestimated his ability to withstand her departure in Paris, but how crushingly it affected his spirit. The man who, four years earlier, said of the Nazis, "I left a note in my apartment; they'll know where to find me," is now a handful of pulp waiting to be tossed away. Though Laszlo, the saint, has won her admiration, Rick's terse admission of his weakness, his humanity, wins her love. . . . How much I loved you, how much I still love you!"

But Rick has a ploy—noble, to be sure—of his own. Ilsa thinks she can stay with Rick and send Laszlo off to convert the masses, so Rick devises several artful decoys. *Someone,* he lets it be known, is going to use those letters of transit to leave Casablanca. Ilsa believes Laszlo will go alone; Renault believes Rick and Ilsa are going; and poor Laszlo believes he and Ilsa will be the lucky pair. Rick tells the truth only to the person he likes least; again, admiration is the operative motive. Rick contributes to The Cause by telling his rival the truth, and prolongs his mistress's love by lying to her. In both cases he is preserving illusions as well as saving lives—and, as regards Ilsa and Laszlo, preserving an illusion about Rick's "gesture" toward Ilsa may be the only way to save their life together.

Rick is as adept as Renault at the multiple ploy. It would appear he is about to make Strasser (and Renault) happy by promising to turn Laszlo over to them; make Ilsa happy by promising to leave with her; make Ferrari happy by selling the saloon—and Sam—to him. Actually, he is making himself happy by fooling all of them. Renault, ever the professional, tries to stop Rick from stepping into selflessness; but throughout the film, we have sensed indications that the Vichy-suave Captain, who shares with Rick a vaguely liberal wartime past, may be just corruptible enough to be bribed into political, if not stylistic, nobility. And so, when Rick dispatches Strasser and sends Ilsa and Laszlo off to the remote continent of North America, Renault orders his gendarme to "round up the usual suspects." True to form, Renault is incorrigibly corrupt: where he once evaded the law for sex, he now evades it for comradeship. As for Rick, his generosity masked the removal of an obsession whose poignancy had degenerated into the dull pain of an abscessed tooth. We have known all along that Rick's nobility consisted mainly in setting spilled glasses aright, asking Germans about the color of his eyes, and squeezing a profit out of a café whose specialties were Molotov cocktails of political intrigue. Renault's order to his gendarme is the password into Rick's exclusive new club: The Order of the Heroic Pragmatist. What better place than the edge of the Sahara, and what better companion than Renault, for "the beginning of a beautiful friendship"?

IV

Like the very best Hollywood films (*Citizen Kane, The Searchers, Psycho*), but unlike works by the European commercial avant-garde, *Casablanca* succeeds as allegory, popular myth, clinical psychology or whatever, *and* as a superb romantic melodrama. The writers and Curtiz don't ruin their epiphanies with overexplicit dialogue or long pauses that give us time to consider double and triple meanings. Superficially, *Casablanca* is another Bogart vehicle, driven at Warners' usual reckless pace, and shifting emotional gears at the climax so we can be sure enough of Bogey's soft-hearted tough-guy to return in a few months for his next picture. Rich as it is—though not terrifyingly deep—the film is so damned entertaining that we don't need the spur of a doctoral thesis or cultural insecurity to prod us to see it again and again. And the script that Koch hastily wrote on the substructure of the earlier Epstein efforts—a job that virtually defines Grace Under Pressue (Hollywood-style)—reads so beautifully that, with its publication, many Casablancaphiles may swear off the torture-seats of the local repertory cinema or the commercial interruptions of TV revivals for a shorter, but no less rewarding, pilgrimage to their nearest bookshelf.

RICHARD CORLISS is the film critic for *Time* magazine. The author of *Talking Pictures* (1985, Overlook), he has written widely on film.

ROGER EBERT

CASABLANCA AT FIFTY

THE KEY PASSAGES in *Casablanca* of course are the ones that immediately follow the unexpected entrance of Ingrid Bergman, as Ilsa, into Rick's place. These are unusual among classic movie scenes in being more emotionally affecting on subsequent viewings than they are the first time, and indeed *Casablanca* is one of those rare films that actually improves with repeated viewings.

The first time we see the film we know nothing of the great love affair between Rick and Ilsa in Paris, and so we are simply following along, and the byplay between Ilsa and Sam has still to be decoded. We know it means something, but as yet we don't fully understand it. Then the film continues, and we experience the memories of Paris, we understand the depth of Ilsa's feelings, and the movie sweeps on to its magnificent conclusion. The *next* time we see it, every word between Ilsa and Sam, every nuance, every look or averted glance, has a poignant meaning. It is a good enough scene the first time we see it, but a great scene the second time.

In a sense the whole movie demands the same kind of repeated viewings. Find, if you can, someone who has never seen it, and sit next to your friend during the film. You will almost certainly find yourself more involved than your companion. Your friend is not an insensitive boor; he simply does not understand, as you do, the infinite gradations of poignancy to be found behind every look, and overheard in every line. And in a first viewing he may not even pick up on some of the film's quieter asides, such as the subplot involving the young woman who will do anything to help her husband get out of Casablanca.

If familiarity makes the movie more effective, it also exposes some weaknesses than are not at first apparent. There came a time, in my history with *Casablanca*, when I realized that I did not like Victor Laszlo, the Paul Henreid character, very much. He is a heroic leader of the Resistance, but he has no humor and no resilience. If in peacetime he finds himself in political office, I believe he will be most comfortable in a totalitarian regime. When at the end of the film Rick tells a lie about what happened between himself and Ilsa, in order to preserve Ilsa's image in Laszlo's eyes, Laszlo hardly seems to care. In fact, I think he hardly deserves Ilsa. Rick tells her that her place is at Victor's side, but does Victor notice her there, or need her there? In the long run he is married to his career and his heroism, and there will be more nights when she hears ''As Time Goes By'' and realizes she made a mistake when she got on that airplane.

Of course *Casablanca* is not about love anyway, but about nobility. Set at a time when it seemed possible that the Nazis would overrun civilization, it seriously argues that the problems of a few little people don't amount to a hill of beans. The great break between *Casablanca* and almost all Hollywood love stories—even wartime romances—is that it does not believe love can, or should, conquer all. As I analyze my own feelings about the small handful of movies that affect me emotionally, I find that I am hardly ever moved by love, but often moved by self-sacrifice.

Like everyone who deeply cares for movies, I identify with many of the characters more than I might want to admit. In *Casablanca*, I identify with Rick, and what moves me is not his love for Ilsa but his ability to put a higher good above that love. The Henreid character is a pig because he wants to have his cake and eat it too. What kind of a serious resistance fighter would drag a woman around with him, placing her and his work in unnecessary danger, unless his ego required her adoration? A true hero would have insisted on leaving alone, both for the good of his work and for the happiness of the woman he loves. Laszlo is so blind he does not even understand what exists between Rick and Ilsa. The movie makes a halfhearted attempt to show that Ilsa loves both men, but we can read her heart.

Bogart has never been more touching than as he sits alone with his bottle and his cigarette, drenched in self-pity. The cruelty with which he assaults Ilsa after she walks back into the empty club is all the more painful because it is masochistic; talking that way hurts Rick himself much more than it hurts her. He is tearing at an open wound. She is a little slow to understand, but then one of the screenplay's subtle qualities is that Ilsa is always a beat behind what is really happening. If it is true, as legend has it, that the ending of the movie was not written until the last day, and that Bergman never knew which of the two men Ilsa would end up with, this may explain her air of being slightly dazed. This subtle confusion in the face of a man she loves is one of Bergman's strongest qualities as an actress, anyway, as we can see in Hitchcock's *Notorious*, a film with a buried theme remarkably similar to *Casablanca*.

The direction of Michael Curtiz is remarkable for being completely economical. He creates a picture we would be hard-pressed to improve, and does it without calling attention to the fact that it has been directed at all. Mostly he uses the basic repertory of cinematic story-telling, as encoded by Griffith and rehearsed in thousands of earlier films: Establishing shot, movement, medium shots, alternating closeups, POV shots, reactions. Is there a single shot that calls attention to itself for its own sake? I cannot think of one (there are dozens in *Citizen Kane*). Curtiz is at the service of the characters and the story. Nobody ever asks "Remember that great shot in *Casablanca*?" because there are no great shots in *Casablanca*. If they think there are, they were misinformed.

Howard Hawks, asked for his definition of a great movie, said: "Three great scenes, no bad scenes." *Casablanca* multiplies his formula by four.

ROGER EBERT is the Pulitzer Prize-winning film critic of the *Chicago Sun Times* and the co-host of the TV program "Siskel & Ebert." He is the author of *Roger Ebert's Movie Home Companion* (Andrews & McMeel) as well as numerous other books.

251

UMBERTO ECO

CASABLANCA: CULT MOVIES AND INTERTEXTUAL COLLAGE

CULT

"WAS THAT ARTILLERY FIRE, or is it my heart pounding?" Whenever *Casablanca* is shown, at this point the audience reacts with an enthusiasm usually reserved for football. Sometimes a single word is enough: Fans cry every time Bogey says "kid." Frequently the spectators quote the best lines before the actors say them.

According to traditional standards in aesthetics, *Casablanca* is not a work of art, if such an expression still has a meaning. In any case, if the films of Dreyer, Eisenstein, or Antonioni are works of art, *Casablanca* represents a very modest aesthetic achievement. It is a hodgepodge of sensational scenes strung together implausibly, its characters are psychologically incredible, its actors act in a mannered way. Nevertheless, it is a great example of cinematic discourse, a palimpsest for future students of twentieth-century religiosity, a paramount laboratory for semiotic research into textual strategies. Moreover, it has become a cult movie.

What are the requirements for transforming a book or a movie into a cult object? The work must be loved, obviously, but this is not enough. It must provide a completely furnished world so that its fans can quote characters and episodes as if they were aspects of the fan's private sectarian world, a world about which one can make up quizzes and play trivia games so that the adepts of the sect recognize through each other a shared expertise. Naturally all these elements (characters and episodes) must have some archetypical appeal, as we shall see. One can ask and answer questions about the various subway stations of New York or Paris only if these spots have become or have been assumed as mythical areas and such names as Canarsie Line or Vincennes-Neuilly stand not only for physical places but become the catalyzers of collective memories.

Curiously enough, a book can also inspire a cult even though it is a great work of art: Both *The Three Musketeers* and *The Divine Comedy* rank among the cult books; and there are more trivia games among the fans of Dante than among the fans of Dumas. I suspect that a cult movie, on the contrary, must display some organic imperfections: It seems that the boastful *Rio Bravo* is a cult movie and the great *Stagecoach* is not.

I think that in order to transform a work into a cult object one must be able to break, dislocate, unhinge it so that one can remember only parts of it, irrespective of their original relationship with the whole. In the case of a book one can unhinge it, so to speak, physically, reducing it to a series of excerpts. A movie, on the contrary, must be already ramshackle, rickety, unhinged in itself. A perfect movie, since it cannot be reread every time we want, from the point we choose, as happens with a book, remains in our memory as a whole, in the form of a central idea or emotion; only an unhinged movie survives as a disconnected series of images, of peaks, of visual icebergs. It should display not one central idea but many. It should not reveal a coherent philosophy of composition. It must live on, and because of, its glorious ricketiness.

However, it must have some quality. Let me say that it can be ramshackle from the production point of view (in that nobody knew exactly what was going to be done next)—as happened evidently with the *Rocky Horror Picture Show*—but it must display certain textual features, in the sense that, outside the conscious control of its creators, it becomes a sort of textual syllabus, a living example of living textuality. Its addressee must suspect it is not true that works are created by their authors. Works are created by works, texts are created by texts, all together they speak to each other independently of the intention of their authors. A cult movie is the proof that, as literature comes from literature, cinema comes from cinema.

Which elements, in a movie, can be separated from the whole and adored for themselves? In order to go on with this analysis of *Casablanca* I should use some important semiotic categories, such as the ones (provided by the Russian Formalists) of theme and motif. I confess I find it very difficult to ascertain what the various Russian Formalists meant by motif. If—as Veselovsky says—a motif is the simplest narrative unit, then one wonders why ''fire from heaven'' should belong to the same category as ''the persecuted maid'' (since the former can be represented by an image, while the latter requires a certain narrative development). It would be interesting to follow Tomashevsky and to look in *Casablanca* for free or tied and for dynamic or static motifs. We should distinguish between more or less universal narrative functions à la Propp, visual stereotypes like the Cynic Adventurer, and more complex archytypical situations like the Unhappy Love. I hope someone will do this job, but here I will assume, more prudently (and borrowing the concept from research into Artificial Intelligence) the more flexible notion of ''frame.''

In *The Role of the Reader* I distinguished between common and intertextual frames. I meant by ''common frame'' data-structures for representing stereotyped situations such as dining at a restaurant or going to the railway station; in other words, a sequence of actions more or less coded by our normal experience. And by ''intertextual frames'' I meant stereotyped situations derived from preceding textual tradition and recorded by our encyclopedia, such as, for example, the standard duel between the sheriff and the bad guy or the narrative situation in which the hero fights the villain and wins, or more macroscopic textual situations, such as the story of the *vierge souillée* or the classic recognition scene (Bakhtin considered it a motif, in the sense of a chronotope). We could distinguish between stereotyped intertextual frames (for instance, the Drunkard Redeemed by Love) and stereotyped iconographical units (for instance, the Evil Nazi). But since even these iconographical units, when they appear in a movie, if they do not directly elicit an action, at least suggest its possible development, we can use the notion of intertextual frame to cover both.

Moreover, we are interested in finding those frames that not only are recognizable by the audience as belonging to a sort of ancestral intertextual tradition but that also display a particular fascination. "A suspect who eludes a passport control and is shot by the police" is undoubtedly an intertextual frame but it does not have a "magic" flavor. Let me address intuitively the idea of "magic" frame. Let me define as "magic" those frames that, when they appear in a movie and can be separated from the whole, transform this movie into a cult object. In *Casablanca* we find more intertextual frames than "magic" intertextual frames. I will call the latter "intertextual archetypes."

The term "archetype" does not claim to have any particular psychoanalytic or mythic connotation, but serves only to indicate a preestablished and frequently reappearing narrative situation, cited or in some way recycled by innumerable other texts and provoking in the addressee a sort of intense emotion accompanied by the vague feeling of a déjà vu that everybody yearns to see again. I would not say that an intertextual archetype is necessarily "universal." It can belong to a rather recent textual tradition, as with certain topoi of slapstick comedy. It is sufficient to consider it as a topos or standard situation that manages to be particularly appealing to a given cultural area or a historical period.

THE MAKING OF *CASABLANCA*

"Can I tell you a story?" Ilsa asks. Then she adds: "I don't know the finish yet."

Rick says: "Well, go on, tell it. Maybe one will come to you as you go along."

Rick's line is a sort of epitome of *Casablanca* itself. According to Ingrid Bergman, the film was apparently being made up at the same time that it was being shot. Until the last moment not even Michael Curtiz knew whether Ilsa would leave with Rick or with Victor, and Ingrid Bergman seems so fascinatingly mysterious because she did not know at which man she was to look with greater tenderness.

This explains why, in the story, she does not, in fact, choose her fate: She is chosen.

When you don't know how to deal with a story, you put stereotyped situations in it because you know that they, at least, have already worked elsewhere. Let us take a marginal but revealing example. Each time Laszlo orders something to drink (and it happens four times) he changes his choice: (1) Cointreau, (2) cocktail, (3) cognac, and (4) whisky (he once drinks champagne but he does not ask for it). Why such confusing and confused drinking habits for a man endowed with an ascetic temper? There is no psychological reason. My guess is that each time Curtiz was simply quoting, unconsciously, similar situations in other movies and trying to provide a reasonably complete repetition of them.

Thus one is tempted to read *Casablanca* as T. S. Eliot read *Hamlet*, attributing its fascintion not to the fact that it was a successful work (actually he considered it one of Shakespeare's less fortunate efforts) but to the imperfection of its composition. He viewed *Hamlet* as the result of an unsuccessful fusion of several earlier versions of the story, and so the puzzling ambiguity of the main character was due to the author's difficulty in putting together different topoi. So both public and critics find *Hamlet* beautiful because it is interesting, but believe it is interesting because it is beautiful.

On a smaller scale the same thing happened to *Casablanca*. Forced to improvise a plot, the authors mixed a little of everything, and everything they chose came from a repertoire that had stood the test of time. When only a few of these formulas are used, the result is simply kitsch. But when the repertoire of stock formulas is used wholesale, then the result is an architecture like Gaudi's Sagrada Familia: the same vertigo, the same stroke of genius.

STOP BY STOP

Every story involves one or more archetypes. To make a good story a single archetype is usually enough. But *Casablanca* is not satisfied with that. It uses them all.

It would be nice to identify our archetypes scene by scene and shot by shot, stopping the tape at every relevant step. Every time I have scanned *Casablanca* with very cooperative research groups, the review has taken many hours. Furthermore, when a team starts this kind of game, the instances of stopping the videotape increase proportionally with the size of the audience. Each member of the team sees something that the others have missed, and many of them start to find in the movie even memories of movies made after *Casablanca*—evidently the normal situation for a cult movie, suggesting that perhaps the best deconstructive readings should be made of unhinged texts (or that deconstruction is simply a way of breaking up texts).

However, I think that the first twenty minutes of the film represent a sort of review of the principal archetypes. Once they have been assembled, without any synthetic concern, then the story starts to suggest a sort of savage syntax of the archetypical elements and organizes them in multileveled oppositions. *Casablanca* looks like a musical piece with an extraordinarily long overture, where every theme is exhibited according to a monodic line. Only later does the symphonic work take place. In a way the first twenty minutes could be analyzed by a Russian Formalist and the rest by a Greimasian.

Let me then try only a sample analysis of the first part. I think that a real text-analytical study of *Casablanca* is still to be made, and I offer only some hints to future teams of researchers, who will carry out, someday, a complete reconstruction of its deep textual structure.

1. First, African music, then the *Marseillaise.* Two different genres are evoked: adventure movie and patriotic movie.

2. Third genre. The globe: Newsreel. The voice even suggests the news report. Fourth genre: the odyssey of refugees. Fifth genre: Casablanca and Lisbon are, traditionally, *hauts lieux* for international intrigues. Thus in two minutes five genres are evoked.

3. Casablanca–Lisbon. Passage to the Promised Land (Lisbon–America). Casablanca is the Magic Door. We still do not know what the Magic Key is or by which Magic Horse one can reach the Promised Land.

4. "Wait, wait, wait." To make the passage one must submit to a Test. The Long Expectation. Purgatory situation.

5. "Deutschland über Alles." The German anthem introduces the theme of Barbarians.

6. The Casbah. Pépé le Moko. Confusion, robberies, violence, and repression.

7. Pétain (Vichy) vs. the Cross of Lorraine. See at the end the same opposition closing the story: Eau de Vichy vs. Choice of the Resistance. War Propaganda movie.

8. The Magic Key: the visa. It is around the winning of the Magic Key that passions are unleashed. Captain Renault mentioned: He is the Guardian of the Door, or the boatman of the Acheron to be conquered by a Magic Gift (money or sex).

9. The Magic Horse: the airplane. The airplane flies over Rick's Café Américain, thus recalling the Promised Land of which the Café is the reduced model.

10. Major Strasser shows up. Theme of the Barbarians, and their emasculated slaves. "Je suis l'empire à la fin de la décadence/

Qui regarde passer les grands barbares blancs/En composant des acrostiques indolents...."

11. "Everybody comes to Rick's." By quoting the original play, Renault introduces the audience to the Café. The interior: Foreign Legion (each character has a different nationality and a different story to tell, and also his own skeleton in the closet), Grand Hotel (people come and people go, and nothing ever happens), Mississippi River Boat, New Orleans Brothel (Black piano player), the Gambling Inferno in Macao or Singapore (with Chinese women), the Smugglers' Paradise, the Last Outpost on the Edge of the Desert. Rick's place is a magic circle where everything can happen—love, death, pursuit, espionage, games of chance, seductions, music, patriotism. Limited resources and the unit of place, due to the theatrical origin of the story, sudggested an admirable condensation of events in a single setting. One can identify the usual paraphernalia of at least ten exotic genres.

12. Rick slowly shows up, first by synecdoche (his hand), then by metonymy (the check). The various aspects of the contradictory (plurifilmic) personality of Rick are introduced: the Fatal Adventurer, the Self-Made Businessman (money is money), the Tough Guy from a gangster movie, Our Man in Casablanca (international intrigue), the Cynic. Only later he will be characterized also as the Hemingwayan Hero (he helped the Ethiopians and the Spaniards against fascism). He does not drink. This undoubtedly represents a nice problem, for later Rick must play the role of the Redeemed Drunkard and he has to be made a drunkard (as a Disillusioned Lover) so that he can be redeemed. But Bogey's face sustains rather well this unbearable number of contradictory psychological features.

13. The Magic Key, in person: the transit letters. Rick receives them from Peter Lorre and from this moment everybody wants them: how to avoid thinking of Sam Spade and of *The Maltese Falcon*?

14. Music Hall. Mr. Ferrari. Change of genre: comedy with

brilliant dialogue. Rick is now the Disenchanted Lover, or the Cynical Seducer.

15. Rick vs. Renault. The Charming Scoundrels.

16. The theme of the Magic Horse and the Promised Land returns.

17. Roulette as the Game of Life and Death (Russian Roulette that devours fortunes and can destroy the happiness of the Bulgarian Couple, the Epiphany of Innocence). The Dirty Trick: cheating at cards. At this point the Trick is an Evil one but later it will be a Good one, providing a way to the Magic Key for the Bulgarian bride.

18. Arrest and tentative escape of Ugarte. Action movie.

19. Laszlo and Ilsa. The Uncontaminated Hero and La Femme Fatale. Both in white—always; clever opposition with Germans, usually in black. In the meeting at Laszlo's table, Strasser is in white, in order to reduce the opposition. However, Strasser and Ilsa are Beauty and the Beast. The Norwegian agent: spy movie.

20. The Desperate Lover and Drink to Forget.

21. The Faithful Servant and his Beloved Master. Don Quixote and Sancho.

22. Play it (again, Sam). Anticipated quotation of Woody Allen.

23. The long flashback begins. Flashback as a content and flashback as a form. Quotation of the flashback as a topical stylistic device. The Power of Memory. Last Day in Paris. Two Weeks in Another Town. Brief Encounter. French movie of the 1930's (the station as *quai des brumes*).

24. At this point the review of the archetypes is more or less complete. There is still the moment when Rick plays the Diamond in the Rough (who allows the Bulgarian bride to win), and two typical situations: the scene of the *Marseillaise* and the two lovers discovering that Love Is Forever. The gift to the Bulgarian bride (along with the enthusiasm of the waiters), the *Marseillaise*, and the Love Scene are three instances of the rhetorical figure of Climax, as the

quintessence of Drama (each climax coming obviously with its own anticlimax).

Now the story can elaborate upon its elements.

The first symphonic elaboration comes with the second scene around the roulette table. We discover for the first time that the Magic Key (that everybody believed to be only purchasable with money) can in reality be given only as a Gift, a reward for Purity. the Donor will be Rick. He gives (free) the visa to Laszlo. In reality there is also a third Gift, the Gift Rick makes of his own desire, sacrificing himself. Note that there is no gift for Ilsa, who, in some way, even though innocent, has betrayed two men. The Receiver of the Gift is the Uncontaminated Laszlo. By becoming the Donor, Rick meets Redemption. No one impure can reach the Promised Land. But Rick and Renault redeem themselves and can reach the other Promised Land, not America (which is Paradise) but the Resistance, the Holy War (which is a glorious Purgatory). Laszlo flies directly to Paradise because he has already suffered the ordeal of the underground. Rick, moreover, is not the only one who accepts sacrifice: The idea of sacrifice pervades the whole story, Ilsa's sacrifice in Paris when she abaondons the man she loves to return to the wounded hero, the Bulgarian bride's sacrifice when she is prepared to give herself to help her husband, Victor's sacrifice when he is prepared to see Ilsa with Rick to guarantee her safety.

The second symphonic elaboration is upon the theme of the Unhappy Love. Unhappy for Rick, who loves Ilsa and cannot have her. Unhappy for Ilsa, who loves Rick and cannot leave with him. Unhappy for Victor, who understands that he has not really kept Ilsa. The interplay of unhappy loves produces numerous twists and turns. In the beginning Rick is unhappy because he does not understand why Ilsa leaves him. Then Victor is unhappy because he does not understand why Ilsa is attracted to Rick. Finally Ilsa is unhappy because she does not understand why Rick makes her leave with her husband.

These unhappy loves are arranged in a triangle. But in the normal adulterous triangle there is a Betrayed Husband and a Victorious Lover, while in this case both men are betrayed and suffer a loss.

In this defeat, however, an additional element plays a part, so subtly that it almost escapes the level of consciousness. Quite subliminally a hint of Platonic Love is established. Rick admires Victor, Victor is ambiguously attracted by the personality of Rick, and it seems that at a certain point each of the two is playing out the duel of sacrifice to please the other. In any case, as in Rousseau's *Confessions*, the woman is here an intermediary between the two men. She herself does not bear any positive value (except, obviously, Beauty): The whole story is a virile affair, a dance of seduction between Male Heroes.

From now on the film carries out the definitive construction of its intertwined triangles, to end with the solution of the Supreme Sacrifice and of the Redeemed Bad Guys. Note that, while the redemption of Rick has long been prepared, the redemption of Renault is absolutely unjustified and comes only because this was the final requirement the movie had to meet in order to be a perfect Epos of Frames.

THE ARCHETYPES HOLD A REUNION

Casablanca is a cult movie precisely because all the archetypes are there, because each actor repeats a part played on other occasions, and because human beings live not "real" life but life as stereotypically portrayed in previous films. *Casablanca* carries the sense of déjà vu to such a degree that the addressee is ready to see in it what happened after it as well. It is not until *To Have and Have Not* that Bogey plays the role of the Hemingway hero, but here he appears "already" loaded with Hemingwayesque connotations simply because Rick fought in Spain. Peter Lorre trails reminiscences of Fritz Lang, Conrad Veidt's German officer emanates a faint whiff of *The Cabinet of Dr. Caligari*. He is not a ruthless, technological Nazi; he is a nocturnal and diabolical Caesar.

Casablanca became a cult movie because it is not *one* movie. It is "movies." And this is the reason it works, in defiance of any aesthetic theory.

For it stages the powers of Narrativity in its natural state, before art intervenes to tame it. This is why we accept the way that characters change mood, morality, and psychology from one moment to the next, that conspirators cough to interrupt the conversation when a spy is approaching, that bar girls cry at the sound of the *Marseillaise*...

When all the archetypes burst out shamelessly, we plumb Homeric profundity. Two clichés make us laugh but a hundred clichés move us because we sense dimly that the clichés are talking among themselves, celebrating a reunion.

Just as the extreme of pain meets sensual pleasure, and the extreme of perversion borders on mystical energy, so too the extreme of banality allows us to catch a glimpse of the Sublime.

Nobody would have been able to achieve such a cosmic result intentionally. Nature has spoken in place of men. This, alone, is a phenomenon worthy of veneration.

THE CHARGED CULT

The structure of *Casablanca* helps us understand what happens in later movies *born in order to become cult objects.*

What *Casablanca* does unconsciously, other movies will do with extreme intertextual awareness, assuming also that the addressee is equally aware of their purposes. These are "postmodern" movies, where the quotation of the topos is recognized as the only way to cope with the burden of our filmic encyclopedic expertise.

Think for instance of *Bananas*, with its explicit quotation of the Odessa steps from Eisenstein's *Potemkin*. In *Casablanca* one enjoys quotation even though one does not recognize it, and those who recognize it feel as if they all belonged to the same little clique. In

Bananas those who do not catch the topos cannot enjoy the scene and those who do simply feel smart.

Another (and different) case is the quotation of the topical duel between the black Arab giant with his scimitar and the unprotected hero, in *Raiders of the Lost Ark*. If you remember, the topos suddenly turns into another one, and the unprotected hero becomes in a second *The Fastest Gun in the West*. Here the ingenuous viewer can miss the quotation though his enjoyment will then be rather slight; and real enjoyment is reserved for the people accustomed to cult movies, who know the whole repertoire of ''magic'' archetypes. In a way, *Bananas* works for cultivated ''cinephiles'' while *Raiders* works for *Casablanca*-addicts.

The third case is that of *E.T.*, when the alien is brought outside in a Halloween disguise and meets the dwarf coming from *The Empire Strikes Back*. You remember that E.T. starts and runs to cheer him (or it). Here nobody can enjoy the scene if he does not share, at least, the following elements of intertextual competence:

(1) He must know where the second character comes from (Spielberg citing Lucas),

(2) He must know something about the links between the two directors, and

(3) He must know that both monsters have been designed by Rambaldi and that, consequently, they are linked by some form of brotherhood.

The required expertise is not only intercinematic, it is intermedia, in the sense that the addressee must know not only other movies but all the mass media gossip about movies. This third example presupposes a ''*Casablanca* universe'' in which cult has become the normal way of enjoying movies. Thus in this case we witness an instance of metacult, or of cult about cult—a Cult Culture.

It would be semiotically uninteresting to look for quotations of archetypes in *Raiders* or in *Indiana Jones*: They were conceived within a metasemiotic culture, and what the semiotician can find in them is exactly what the directors put there. Spielberg and Lucas are semiotically nourished authors working for a culture of instinctive semioticians.

With *Casablanca* the situation is different. So *Casablanca* explains *Raiders*, but *Raiders* does not explain *Casablanca*. At most it can explain the new ways in which *Casablanca* will be received in the next years.

It will be a sad day when a too smart audience will read *Casablanca* as conceived by Michael Curtiz after having read Calvino and Barthes. But that day will come. Perhaps we have been able to discover here, for the last time, the Truth.

Après nous, le déluge.

UMBERTO ECO is professor of semiotics at the University of Bologna, a philosopher, historian, literary critic, and novelist. He lives in Milan.

ROUND UP
THE USUAL SUSPECTS

CASABLANCA is my favorite movie. As a child of World War II, I find its blend of romance and sacrifice irresistible. What I wasn't aware of until two years ago when I started writing a book on the making and meaning of the movie was how fragile it was. Movies made under the studio system were accumulations of accidents, and *Casablanca* was no exception. The cinematographer and film editor were the ones who happened to be available that week. Producer Hal Walls wanted James Wong Howe to photograph the movie and was given Arthur Edeson. Director Mike Curtiz asked for George Amy as his cutter and was given Owen Marks.

Despite a press release sent out by Warner Bros. in January, 1942, there was never any question that Humphrey Bogart would be the star of *Casablanca*. The publicity department sent out hundreds of press releases each week. Many of them, including the release that Ronald Reagan would star in *Casablanca*, were simply a way of getting the names of the studio's contract players into print. The movie was written for Bogart. But the rest of the cast could have been quite different. The first choice for heroic Victor Laszlo was Philip Dorn. Felix Bressart turned down the role played by S.Z. Sakall. And Michele Morgan might well have been chosen to play Ilsa Lund if she hadn't asked for $55,000. "There is no reason in the world for demanding this kind of money for anyone as little known as Michele Morgan,'' Wallis wrote to Curtiz. Wallis could—and did—borrow Ingrid Bergman from David O. Selznick for $25,000. But a choice that seems inevitable in 1992 is only clear because of hindsight. Both the young Swedish actress and the young French actress had been successful in their first American movies. It was *Casablanca* that made Ingrid Bergman a star. Would it have done the same for Michele Morgan who made a fine debut in *Joan of Paris* but whose Hollywood career ended after three films?

A classic movie is the biggest accident of all. A thousand things have to fit together. Fifty years after *Casablanca* was made, I cannot listen to ''The Marseillaise'' drowning out ''Watch on the Rhine'' without feeling stirred. I cannot watch Bogart and Bergman say goodbye at the airport without feeling the bittersweet tug of lost possibilities. So, for me, *Casablanca* is still alive.

ALJEAN HARMETZ is the author of *Round Up The Usual Suspects: Hollywood, World War II and Casablanca* (1992, Hyperion) and of *The Making of The Wizard of Oz* (1977, Knopf). She covered the film industry for *The New York Times* from 1978 to 1990.

J. HOBERMAN

ON CASABLANCA

IN *CASABLANCA* THE WORLD IS a movie set (with a few newsreel cutaways) and America is shown as the universal refuge—or at least Hollywood is. Humphrey Bogart and Dooley Wilson are just about the only real Americans in the cast (another version of Huck and Jim). The rest are all foreigners—Ingrid Bergman, Claude Rains, Sydney Greenstreet—lucky to be spending the war in Culver City. Most of these were even actual refugees from fascism—Paul Henreid, Peter Lorre, Marcel Dalio, S. Z. Sakall, Curt Bois, and, of course, Conrad Veidt as the villainous Nazi, playing out his own version of *From Caligari to Hitler* by climaxing a career that began with the role of Cesare the Somnambulist.

That Lorre, Sakall, and director Michael Curtiz were all born in Hungary can't, of itself, account for the movie's popularity in that country where, I'm told, it is traditionally telecast on New Year's Eve. This casbah is universal. If any Hollywood movie exemplifies the ''genius of the system,'' it is surely *Casablanca*—a film whose success was founded on almost as many types of skill as varieties of luck. (It's ironic that aspiring screenwriters take *Casablanca*'s script as a text; rewritten many times, the film was virtually made up as its makers went along.) Mixing genres with mad abandon, *Casablanca* became a cult film precisely because as Umberto Eco put it, ''it is not *one* movie. It is 'movies'.'' All Hollywood movies that is, with a *soupçon* of the French cinema of the late '30s. In other words, *Casablanca* was the culture of the West, everything we were fighting for in World War II, brought together in one neat package.

It is because *Casablanca* is "movies" that it continues to haunt Hollywood. The film was replicated throughout the '40s and into the Cold War—reaching its nadir with the 1951 *Hong Kong* in which Ronald Reagan (once, according to a Warner Bros. press release, a candidate for the original cast) plays the cynical American adventurer with the secret heart of gold. Ten years later, *Casablanca* was enshrined in revival houses across America as a sacred relic, not to mention an audience-participation precursor of *The Rocky Horror Picture Show*. (Like *Casablanca*, *The Rocky Horror Picture Show* is a compendium of mass media cliché and romantic wisdom—in this case pertaining to post-Elvis Anglo-American youth culture.) If *Casablanca* itself was the *Casablanca* of 1961 (call this now designated cult film "*Casablanca*"), the next decade was, of course, a problematic one for Americans abroad: You might argue Dennis Hopper's *The Last Movie* as the *Casablanca* of 1971, if not for Woody Allen's half-nerdy, half-swinging refetishization of "*Casablanca*," *Play It Again, Sam*.

Perhaps each generation gets the *Casablanca* remake it deserves. Steven Spielberg's *Raiders of the Lost Ark* (1981)—which, in a self-conscious attempt to be "movies," knowingly reshuffled elements of *Casablanca* and "*Casablanca*"—heralded America's reborn confidence and self-absorption. Sidney Pollack's quickly-forgotten *Havana* (1990)—which proposed Robert Redford as the cynical expatriate and Lena Olin as the Swedish dame of mystery, transposing *Casablanca* to the Pearl of the Antilles on the eve of the Castro revolution—is redolent of our current confusion and decline.

J. HOBERMAN is the film critic for the *Village Voice* and the author of numerous books on film, including *Bridge of Light: Yiddish Film Between Two Worlds* (1991, Pantheon); *Vulgar Modernism: Writing on the Movies and Other Media* (1991, Temple University Press) and a co-author of *Midnight Movies* (revised edition 1991, DaCapo).

ORIGINAL REVIEWS

HOWARD BARNES
BOSLEY CROWTHER

from *The New York Times*

ON THE SCREEN

BY HOWARD BARNES

"Casablanca"—Hollywood

"CASABLANCA." a screenplay by Julius J. and Philp G. Epstein and Howard Koch, from a play by Murray Burnett and Joan Alison, directed by Michael Curtiz, produced by Hal B. Wallis, presented by Warner Bros. Pictures at the Hollywood Theater with the following cast:

Rick	Humphrey Bogart
Ilsa Lund	Ingrid Bergman
Victor Laszlo	Paul Henreid
Captain Louis Renault	Claude Rains
Major Strasser	Conrad Veidt
Senor Ferrari	Sidney Greenstreet
Ugarte	Peter Lorre
Carl, a waiter	S. Z. Sakall
Yvonne	Madeleine Le Beau
Sam	Dooley Wilson
Annina Brandel	Joy Page
Berger	John Qualen
Sascha, a bartender	Leonid Kinskey
Jan	Helmut Dantine
Dark European	Curt Bois
Croupier	Marcel Dalio
Singer	Corinna Mura
Mr. Leuchtag	Ludwig Stossel
Mrs. Leuchtag	Ilka Gruning
Senor Martinez	Charles La Torre
Arab Vendor	Frank Puglia
Abdul	Dan Seymour

The kaleidoscopic events of recent weeks have made "Casablanca" impressively topical. The new picture at the Hollywood Theater keys into the headlines with prophetic insight. It exposes the intrigue, political shilly-shally and anti-Fascist resentment which must have been the background for the present Allied offensive in Northwest Africa. At the same time, it is a smashing and moving melodrama in its own right. Good writing, a brilliant cast and artful direction add up here to a superior show, as well as a significant document.

The casting of this Warner Bros. production has been prodigal. Humphrey Bogart and Sidney Greenstreet, who were so good in "The Maltese Falcon" and "Across the Pacific," are once more on hand to give the production ominous and violent potentialities. Meanwhile, there is Ingrid Bergman, playing the heroine of a war picture with all her appealing authority and beauty. And the lesser parts are filled by such knowing performers as Paul Henreid, Conrad Veidt, Claude Rains, Peter Lorre, John Qualen and S. Z. Sakall.

With such a company, a dull script might have made the grade. The fact is that "Casablanca" has a continuity which is a clear blend of melodrama and meaning. There are preposterous moments in the proceedings, as when an embittered American bistro proprietor in Casablanca permits a leader of the European underground movement to escape with the woman he loves; but the show makes a great deal of sense, in addition to being a striking thriller. It has sustained interest as well as excitement. Put it on your recommended list of current screen entertainments.

Bogart is an old hand at this sort of muted melodrama. He has rarely been more forceful than he is as a disillusioned democrat, fighting the Axis long before the rest of his compatriots. Miss Bergman illuminates every scene in which she appears in the role of a Norwegian beauty who falls in love with an American soldier of fortune, but leaves her erstwhile lover to continue the good fight against Nazi aggression. Henreid, Rains, Lorre, Veidt and the others contribute incisive portraits of the curious human tapestry of a desert city which has sprung into prominence long after the film was made.

Michael Curtiz has not let his players down. He has staged "Casablanca" with power and imagination. There is a memorable scene in which a Gestapo gang starts singing German songs in the saloon of the American soldier of fortune and are drowned out by the "Marseillaise." There are sequences of oblique suspense which add tremendously to the total effect of the melodrama. "Casablanca" happens to be timely. It also happens to be an excellent film.

CASABLANCA; screenplay by Julius J. and Philip G. Epstein and Howard Koch; from
a play by Murray Burnett and Joan Alison; directed by Michael Curtiz; produced by
Hal B. Wallis for Warner Brothers. At the Hollywood.

by BOSLEY CROWTHER

Against the electric background of a sleek café in a North African
port, through which swirls a backwash of connivers, crooks and
fleeing European refugees, the Warner Brothers are telling a rich,
suave, exciting and moving tale in their new film, "Casablanca,"
which came to the Hollywood yesterday. They are telling it in the
high tradition of their hard-boiled romantic-adventure style. And to
make it all the more tempting they have given it a top-notch thriller
cast of Humphrey Bogart, Sidney Greenstreet, Peter Lorre, Conrad
Veidt and even Claude Rains, and have capped it magnificently with
Ingrid Bergman, Paul Henreid and a Negro "find" named Dooley
Wilson.

Yes, indeed, the Warners here have a picture which makes the
spine tingle and the heart take a leap. For once more, as in recent
Bogart pictures, they have turned the incisive trick of draping a tender
love story within the folds of a tight topical theme. They have used
Mr. Bogart's personality, so well established in other brilliant films,
to inject a cold point of tough resistance to evil forces afoot in Europe
today. And they have so combined sentiment, humor and pathos with
taut melodrama and bristling intrigue that the result is a highly entertaining and even inspiring film.

The story, as would be natural, has its devious convolutions of
plot. But mainly it tells of a tough fellow named Rick who runs a
Casablanca café and of what happens (or what happened last
December) when there shows up in his joint one night a girl whom
he had previously loved in Paris in company with a fugitive Czech

patriot. The Nazis are tailing the young Czech; the Vichy officials offer only brief refuge—and Rick holds the only two sure passports which will guarantee his and the girl's escape. But Rick loves the girl very dearly, she is now married to this other man—and whenever his Negro pianist sits there in the dark and sings "As Time Goes By" that old, irresistible feeling consumes him in a choking, maddening wave.

Don't worry; we won't tell you how it all comes out. That would be rankest sabotage. But we will tell you that the urbane detail and the crackling dialogue which has been packed into this film by the scriptwriters, the Epstein brothers and Howard Koch, is of the best. We will tell you that Michael Curtiz has directed for slow suspense and that his camera is always conveying grim tension and uncertainty. Some of the significant incidents, too, are affecting—such as that in which the passionate Czech patriot rouses the customers in Rick's café to drown out a chorus of Nazis by singing the "Marseillaise," or any moment in which Dooley Wilson is remembering past popular songs in a hushed room.

We will tell you also that the performances of the actors are all of the first order, but especially those of Mr. Bogart and Miss Bergman in the leading roles. Mr. Bogart is, as usual, the cool, cynical, efficient and super-wise guy as becomes his inner character, and he handles it credibly. Miss Bergman is surpassingly lovely, crisp and natural as the girl and lights the romantic passages with a warm and genuine glow.

Mr. Rains is properly slippery and crafty as a minion of Vichy perfidy, and Mr. Veidt plays again a Nazi officer with cold and implacable resolve. Very little is demanded of Mr. Greenstreet as a shrewd black-market trader, but that is good, and Mr. Henreid is forthright and simple as the imperiled Czech patriot. Mr. Wilson's performance as Rick's devoted friend, though rather brief, is filled with a sweetness and compassion which lend a helpful mood to the whole film, and other small roles are played ably by S. Z. Sakall, Joy Page, Leonid Kinskey and Mr. Lorre.

In short, we will say that "Casablanca" is one of the year's most

exciting and trenchant films. It certainly won't make Vichy happy—
but that's just another point for it.